MY FATHER,
THE GERMANS
AND I

THE
SEAGULL
LIBRARY OF
GERMAN
LITERATURE

JUREK BECKER

MY FATHER, THE GERMANS AND I

essays, lectures, interviews

EDITED BY CHRISTINE BECKER

LONDON NEW YORK CALCUTTA

This publication was supported by a grant
from the Goethe-Institut India

Seagull Books, 2021

Mein Judentum
Widerstand in 'Jakob der Lügner'
Das Vorstellbare gefällt mir immer besser als das Bekannte
Über die letzten Tage
Mein Vater, die Deutschen und ich
Der Tausendfüßler
Schriftsteller in Ost und Schriftsteller in West
Über den Kulturverfall in unserer Zeit
Über den Wert der bürgerlichen Rechte
Ist der Sozialismus am Ende?
Die unsichtbare Stadt
Zum Bespitzeln gehören zwei
Vom Handwerkszeug der Schriftsteller
Das ist wie ein Gewitter

All essays taken from Jurek Becker, *Mein Vater, die Deutschen und
ich. Aufsätze, Vorträge, Interviews*. Herausgegeben von Christine
Becker. © Suhrkamp Verlag, Frankfurt am Main 2007

First published in English translation by Seagull Books, 2010

ISBN 978 0 8574 2 824 0

British Library Cataloguing-in-Publication Data
A catalogue record for this book is available from the British Library

Typeset by Seagull Books, Calcutta, India
Printed and bound by WordsWorth India, New Delhi, India

CONTENTS

The oeuvre of the German writer Jurek Becker consists of novels, short stories, screenplays and essays, a selection of which is presented in this volume. Becker wrote these texts over a period of twenty years in response to various personal and political events. Some of the texts have already been published in English language journals; others were translated into English for this edition.

It was sheer chance that Jurek Becker became a writer of German in the first place. He was born in Poland to Jewish parents, survived the Ghetto and concentration camps and, at the end of the war, found himself in East Berlin. These origins and this childhood shaped the author's ironic distance to the world, an attitude that became one of the defining characteristics of his work. His first novel *Jacob the Liar*, which was adapted twice for the cinema and made him famous all over the world, caused quite a stir as the public reacted to Becker's unprecedented use of comedy in portraying the tragedy of the Holocaust.

Contemplations about politics and literature in the East and West are at the core of his essays. Although his origins predestined him to be an outsider, Jurek Becker was always passionately involved in the political affairs of the country he was living in—be it East, West or reunified Germany. Being politically involved was, as he once said, part of a healthy lifestyle for him, 'like teeth-brushing'. And it was always his desire to motivate his readers to get involved, to understand political affairs as their very own and to actively shape their future.

The universal question of our existence between assimilation and resistance, a topic in his literary works, is also the focus of his essays. His heritage and his reflections on his own work are also important, albeit less significant, themes.

Humour and irony characterize Jurek Becker's voice, but clarity and precision are also hallmarks of his style. His attitude toward German, the language that eventually became his medium, was shaped by deliberate awareness from the beginning, as it was not his native language. The author's inclination toward lucidity and accuracy in German is matched in the English translations.

Tracy Graves and Martin Bäumel provided considerable assistance in translating, proofreading and helping select texts for the volume. The other texts originate from different translators, among them Becker's son Jonathan—the 'Becker sound' rings through in all of them.

In the past, whenever someone would ask me about my parentage and background, I would answer: 'My parents were Jews.' I used this sentence like a proven formula, one that gives information of unsurpassable clarity. When the asker occasionally confirmed my statement with his own: 'Then you are a Jew,' I would repeat my formula: 'My parents were Jews.' The distinction seemed somehow important to me, although I had never made it a topic for discussion; indeed, it had never even been the subject of thoughts that deserved to be discussed.

Moreover, I cannot ignore the effects that being born into a Jewish family had on my early life. When I was two years old, my parents and I lived in the ghetto in Łódź, which shortly before had been renamed Litzmannstadt. After that, followed periods in the concentration camps at Ravensbrück and

Sachsenhausen. When the war was over, my family—up to then a veritable tribe, I am told—had been reduced to three survivors: my father, an aunt whom I cannot remember because right after the Germans marched in she was able to flee Poland, perhaps to America, and I was the third.

My father, who was in a different camp than I at the end of the war, searched for and found me with the help of an American relief organization. All of my clear and recollectable memories start from this point. I was already seven, nearly eight years old.

I know that other people have childhood memories that reach back much farther than mine. And because I was not satisfied just to know that life takes one path for most people and another path for me, or that something was not functioning right in my brain, I spent a lot of time trying to find the reason for this difference. My success was modest; nevertheless, I must consider the result correct, as long as no one gives me a more plausible explanation. This is how I figure it.

First of all, the unusually late start of my memories must have something to do with repression. A protective mechanism, the presence of which is certainly a blessing, could separate me from a painful period and thus protect me from it. Second, I cannot believe that there is much to remember. The days in a concentration camp pass in grey uneventfulness, interrupted by incidents that could be disturbing only to adults—because they alone saw life being threatened at every turn. For children, the days were bleak and indistinguishable from one another. Third, and finally, I suppose that what I was leading at that time can hardly be called 'life'; it deserved only the term 'existence'. It was a state of dullness and stupor, in which life functions were reduced to a minimum, in which every action was designed solely as a means of survival. There was no room for observation, curiosity, or intellectual meditation. It is likely that everything that took place was of such a nature that the person I was at the time did not consider it worth remembering. These three circumstances—so runs my ultimate conclusion—obliterated from my memory the period of time prior to our release, not so completely, to be sure, that one could say nothing whatever remained, but so thoroughly that the little bit left over could hardly be called memory.

After the war, my father stayed in Berlin with me, again for reasons I can only guess at. For he never wanted to discuss it with me. Not that he was like someone who does not want to reveal a secret; he was more like someone who avoids a question because he does not know the answer himself. I think he had lost his home in the war, to the extent that a home consists primarily of people and not landscapes: of relatives, friends, confidants. They were no longer there, they were dead; the luckiest had disappeared without a trace. So my father proceeded from the premise that if a man feels drawn to no place in particular, he will feel most comfortable staying right where he is.

He alluded to but one of his reasons for staying there, and then only occasionally and indirectly; yet it was enough that I was later able to make sense out of it. He believed that in his old environment, in Poland, anti-Semitism did not appear for the first time when the Germans marched in. And the fewer the number of Jews living there, the greater the chance that people would try to make life difficult for them. Once he said: 'In the end it is not the Polish anti-Semites who have lost the war.' He hoped that the discrimination against the Jews would be most completely done away with in the place where it had taken on its most horrifying expression. And when he died in 1972, he was happily convinced that he had not been wrong on at least this point. He once said: 'If anti-Semitism did not exist—do you think I would have felt like a Jew for a single second?'

At any rate, there I was in Berlin without knowing a word of German. The fact that I did not begin learning German until the age of eight may explain the rather reverent nature of my relationship to this language. Just as other children my age were interested in ladybugs or racing cars, examining them from all angles, I examined words and sentences, turning them over and over. In an intense preoccupation with language I saw the only means of escape—escape from the ridicule and prejudice resulting from my being the only eight-year-old anywhere around who could not speak properly. And I still believe today that there was certainly no other way for me.

Right from the start and very persistently my father avoided bringing any conversation with me around to the past. I never discovered what goal he was trying to achieve with his silence, whether he himself wanted to find peace from the past years, whether his reasons were personal ones, in other words, or whether he wanted to protect me from that period of time. But whichever goal he had in mind, he did not achieve it.

My father rarely went to the synagogue, and then only to meet a few friends. Not friends from before the war, but people who had had similar experiences in concentration camps and with whom he therefore had something in common—to a certain extent. He never took me along, not even when I begged him to. As if going to the synagogue were only for adults. But nevertheless, I know that he would sit and wait impatiently for the service to end, so he could talk with the people he had sought there.

As a result, I have never been in a synagogue. Well, just once, many years later. I went there with a director I had been making a film with. We both wanted to see what it was like, if only to avoid making gross errors in the depiction of Jewish rituals. But never before nor thereafter. I am convinced that this state of affairs is evidence neither of a casual attitude toward religion nor of a tie I may have dissolved. And because what takes place in a synagogue concerns a 'something', whereas my concern is a 'someone', the reasons probably lie within myself.

I never sought out the company and companionship of Jews, nor did I avoid it. I discovered whether someone I knew was a Jew or not only by chance, if at all. If someone intentionally drew my attention to this fact, the same question would always run through my mind: Why is he telling me this? I may even have felt somewhat disgusted. For it seemed to me that the person in question expected me to behave differently toward him, upon learning that he was a Jew, than I would have done normally.

I maintain that belonging to a group of people called 'the Jews' can be perceived only as a voluntary act; it is a choice that can be made in one way or another, in the last analysis an intellectual decision. I have encountered considerable opposition to this view, and at times I have wanted to defend it as fiercely as possible. I do not want to develop this idea beyonq saying: The opponents of such a view come from all over—from the ranks of the believers, such as the Zionists, but also from the ranks of the most embittered anti-Semites, the authors of the race laws, for instance, who during the Third Reich did not want to leave the individual any freedom of choice whatsoever, whether he was Jewish or not.

I still do not know what the characteristics of a Jew are. I do know, however, that others believe they can recognize these traits. I have heard it said that a man is a Jew if his mother is Jewish. Whoever believes that can go right on believing it, but I cannot share this view. A human being is someone whose parents are human beings, nothing more and nothing less.

This disbelief on my part is not the same as if I refused to accept that the moon revolves around the earth or the electron around the nucleus of an atom. For it seems to me that the traits relegating a person to the group called 'Jews' are totally arbitrary, with one exception: Such a person *wants* to belong to it. These traits are related to convictions, either handed down or newly won, as well as to rites and creeds; but in no case are they so constituted that an outsider, who has no idea of the problem's complexity, could identify them right away. Not in the way that a geologist, who has never seen a particular rock, would still be able to say: 'This rock belongs to the category of semiprecious stones.'

I can be a Christian and I can stop being one. And if I work at it stubbornly and long enough, I can also stop being an Italian or a Russian or an American.

How then can withdrawing from Judaism be defined and bound by certain limits, as if by natural laws? I not only cannot believe that, I consider such limits threatening and shocking as well—like a force with such power over me that any protest would be senseless.

It is for this reason that I am devoting so much space to the problem; and this is why I get upset and argumentative and, in the end, aggressive—because people have repeatedly and tediously decided for me who and what I am: among other things, a Jew. It sounds like an occupation to me, or like a reminder to settle an account for guilt that I never ordered. And even if I were prepared to pay up, I would not know how or with what. How do you behave when you are a Jew? When someone says to me: 'Don't worry about it, don't do anything you don't think is right,' I may be soothed, but just temporarily. Because then it seems to me that the man who is counted as a Jew serves only to augment a sum that means nothing to him, or he is supposed to be a tiny weight on a set of scales. And neither would suit me.

However, that is but part of the problem. I know that we are not merely the person we imagine ourselves to be; for better or for worse, we must also be the person others believe us to be. That is the sad part. Seen in this way, I am cursed many times over, because I am the person that many people have obligingly decided I should be: a Jew. I do not want to expend all my strength rebelling against this, nor do I see much point in it. I only know that now, as I steer myself toward my destiny, clenching my teeth, I will disappoint the hopes of some people and confirm the fears of others. Yet, the same thing would happen in the end, against my will, given any other association.

Consequently, what my being a Jew does *not* mean might already be somewhat clearer. In any case, it is not the sense of belonging to a religious community. Because I am an atheist, it seems to me that the Jewish religion is no more insightful than any other; and my interest in this religion—admittedly only a superficial one—has not brought me one step closer to seeing the light. But by all means, it seems to me that Judaism is more successful and more convincing than, for example, the Christian religions, if viewed from a standpoint that might be termed 'literary'. (For such praise, the persons I refer to will surely be most grateful.)

Being a Jew does not arouse a feeling of good for tune because I, willingly or not, belong to an extended group of people who, like other groups of comparable size, accomplish things, both admirable and miserable. I do not feel a surge of pride because Kafka was a Jew, although I suspect that his writings were very significant for me. I do not feel upset because Max Frisch is not a Jew, although he is of similar importance to me. I do not feel ashamed that the Jews in the

Near East have established themselves as a master race (*Herrenmenschen*) and are practising a type of politics that I can only describe as predatory.[1] I just feel angry that people deal with people in such a way.

I cannot offer any information on the question of how great an influence certain people have had on me, or how much incentive they have given me—particularly those for whom Judaism comprises a large part or even the focus of their lives. I do not doubt that such influences and incentives have existed and continue to exist. But I feel it is fruitless to gauge them and measure them against other influences and incentives. Perhaps it would be worse than fruitless, perhaps even belligerent in a certain way.

Once, I recall, we had a visitor from a foreign country. I must have been about eleven years old. My father introduced me to a bearded, balding old man who wore a small cap on his head, the likes of which I had never seen before. My father told him my name, and I held out my hand. But he did not move; he looked at me for a long time and shook his head, barely perceptibly, as if he could not understand something. Then he grabbed me—I was afraid for a moment and struggled—and closed me in his arms. I turned and looked at my father, because I was confused and wanted to know how to behave. My father reassured me by calmly raising his hand, indicating that I should just let it happen, everything was fine. So

I kept still and waited to be released. Then I noticed that the stranger, while drawing me closer and closer, was crying. I looked up at the ceiling, because his body was trembling so. He kept his eyes shut, and tears disappeared into his beard. I had to try very hard to keep from crying myself. I remember that I wanted so much to comfort the man, and only wished to know why. We stood there for what seemed like an eternity. I did not turn to my father again; now I could have stood still for two hours. Then the stranger let me go, mumbled something and left the room. My father and I remained silent until he returned from the bathroom. He said goodbye like someone who had suddenly recalled that he was in a hurry, and he did not look at me again.

When he was gone, I asked my father why the man had cried so. My father told me I was too young to understand. I thought that this was just an excuse, that he could not explain it to me because he did not understand himself. But today I know better.

I never saw the man again. Although I never spoke a word to him, I still cannot forget him. Whenever the word 'Jew' comes up, not as a description of a particular person but rather as an abstract way of distinguishing between people, I think of this man. He has become a sort of symbol for me, however foolish or incomprehensible that may seem to all those who have never been embraced by him or who have never seen him cry. Somehow I sensed that his violent emotion had nothing to do with me as an individual, that it stemmed from an allegiance that had nothing personal about it. I got a hint of this man's ties to something that lay far outside of himself, something more important to him than anything else. And even if I am not in a position to follow him part of the way along this path, I have received something like a message from him, telling me that this path exists and how much it means to some people.

It must be that one's sense of belonging to a group of people is strongest when that group is under attack. In such circumstances, someone who declares that he no longer wishes to belong to this group may easily be considered a deserter, a coward, or an egoist. On the other hand, if peace and its existence does not seem threatened, it is possible that its number will silently and imperceptibly decrease. Dialectics are at work here.

In the area where I grew up, there were no assaults on the group of Jews. Not of the sort I would have noticed, at least, and not of the sort aimed at the Jewishness of people who certainly were something more than just Jews. We all are familiar with the man who cries 'anti-Semitism' at every mention of his misbehaviour. Just as we all are familiar with the government that, when accused of improper conduct, makes 'anti-socialism' its excuse. One really has to be careful.

I simply want to say it is entirely possible that if the Jews of my childhood had been forced to join together and protect themselves, I would have become part of their community as a matter of course. Or it could be that I would have severed my connection with them; that is the other side of the coin. But as I said, there was nothing there that I had to get away from. There were no ties to sever and no mores to abandon. There were no traditions that could have forced me to make a choice—to accept or to reject them. It would have taken a real effort on my part to become a Jew. There was no one who might have sent me along such a path, and I did not do it by myself. For better or for worse, I simply did not do it.

In general, I suppose that traditions mean very little to me. Whenever I observed traditions being preserved, there was usually something present that disturbed me. Even when I saw something that in my opinion truly deserved being preserved. Too often, it seems to me, the disturbing side of tradition manages to gain the upperhand.

As a very young man, there was a time when I loved to go bowling. I joined a bowling league, and it was a lot of fun—up to the point when the bowlers would sit down, order some beer, and start to sing. It was as if this ritual could not be divorced from bowling, and I could not exclude myself from it if I wanted to be accepted as a bowler. It was quite clear to me that some of the men had only become bowlers because of the beer and the singing.

Feeling bound to a tradition is obviously not the same as being exposed to influences; and it is not the same as having gone to a particular school. I can talk about the influences I am conscious of, but I cannot discuss those I am unaware of. They may exist, however.

When my book *Jacob the Liar* was first published, several critics wrote that I found myself therewith in the tradition of Sholem Aleichem and Isaac Bashevis Singer. The truth is that I read Sholem Aleichem for the first time after I had seen the musical 'Fiddler on the Roof', a while after I had written the book. And to this day I have yet to read a single line of Singer. After hearing this, I can imagine someone saying: 'See, that's it! That's precisely the Jew in you that the critics perceived right way. And whether you're aware of it or not, whether you admit it or not—it's there. You can't deny it, just as you can't deny that down is down and blue is blue.'

I suppose that if I am wrong about such an important issue, it would not be the first time. I suppose that I have failed to recognize influences that were very intense, that I have overlooked bonds that were too obvious to miss. I may not have felt like a Jew, but yet I am one in a hundred different ways. So what? For what reason, I ask myself, do I have to get to the

root of this matter? Would I be any smarter afterwards? I am afraid not. I am afraid I would only be
trying in vain to uncover a secret without which my
life would be much poorer.

Translated by Claudia Johnson and Richard A. Zipser

Note

1 In the collection of essays 'Ende des
  Größenwahns' (1996), the author added the following footnote: 'This judgement appears to me as
  excessive and wrong.—J. B.'

Writing is an occupation that does not deserve excessive admiration or mystification. The only secrets connected to literature are the market success of some books, sometimes the book prices as well as literature prizes and sometimes the conclusions critics and literary scholars draw about books. To me, everything else seems to be rational and, therefore, explainable. And it is certainly no mystery that the situation of writers in the East differs from that of writers in the West in the following ways:

> in the different kinds of political engagement of most writers there and here;

> in the discrepancies between the impact of literature there and here;

> in the different kinds of attention literature receives, from both readers and the governmental authorities;

in the different forms of censorship, that is, the various ways a writer is forced to conform;

in the different forms of competition that exist in Eastern and Western markets.

Now, it is not always the case that one understands the conditions of one's own country best, just like one does not necessarily understand an event just because one witnessed it. Sometimes, actually, witnesses know the least. Nevertheless, I want to try to give you an eyewitness report, so to speak, on writing in the East or, to be more precise, in the German Democratic Republic. Even more precisely, when I talk about 'Writers in the GDR', I oftentimes only think of myself. I cannot speak for anyone else; sometimes, I even doubt I have the right to speak for myself. Furthermore, in my report on writing in the East, Western writing will only serve as a standard of comparison, not as an equally important object of investigation. At some points, I will mention it. At others, it will only provide a background for my discussion, a background that you, as Westerners, are already familiar with and that I certainly won't need to talk about. This proportion of information seems only appropriate for a writer from the GDR, such as myself, when talking to an audience in England, as rare as that might be.

I come from a country in which the possibilities of literature are, I am strongly convinced, overrated.

And they are overrated not just by writers. This would somehow be normal, just as it is normal, for example, that someone who produces cuckoo clocks considers cuckoo clocks more important than they really are. What I am talking about is the overestimation of literature by the authorities, by the government, by a ministry, for example, or by the Party, which, for us, is a synonym for 'Communist Party'. The overestimation I am talking about takes both a positive and a negative form. When a book depicts a human being or a group of human beings acting in an ideal way—whatever that might be—the powers that be expect positive consequences for the future. They expect that many readers will take the literary character as an example and act accordingly. Or the opposite happens. For example, when characters object to the policy of the Party, or even when it is clear that the author has such objections, the authorities fear negative consequences. They fear that readers might embrace and adopt these objections and act accordingly. So they promote one kind of literature and cause difficulties for the other kind. This behaviour seems consistent enough, once you accept their premise. Their premise is that a literary character or a literary opinion multiplies after the publication of a work. According to this premise, the reader becomes a pawn and his actions essentially depend on the writer to whom he falls prey.

I find that inappropriate for several reasons. On the one hand, it is not compatible with Marxist views, with the insight that the social existence of men determines their consciousness, that their daily experience counts for more than the insights they might gain from books they read. On the other hand, I simply don't want this view to be right because it is unappealing. I would be very uncomfortable if people could be that easily influenced. Moreover, it doesn't conform with my observations. It would be unbearable for me if writers really had such a dangerous weapon at their disposal. This concept implies an image of humanity that I don't care for and that I cannot accept because it underestimates the individual mind.

Nevertheless, I think that the literature in my country is more effective and of more consequence than the literature of any Western country I know. I contend that in my country, the GDR, writers are indeed powerful people whose work has more impact and causes more of a stir than in most other places in the world. This may seem like a contradiction, but, in reality, the importance of literature in the GDR is artificially created. Or, if it is not artificially created, then it is, at the very least, artificially cultivated, which means that it is contingent on circumstances that result precisely from the overestimation of literature. Let me explain what I mean by this.

When literature is continuously given greater importance or consideration than it actually deserves, when we continuously pretend that our fate is determined by books, a kind of 'feedback loop' is created. That means, if we convince ourselves over and over again that the writers' job is dangerous or useful and, more than that, if we treat writers and the texts they produce accordingly, writers and their books will really become more and more important.

Here is a simple example: A random item is on the market. Let's call it Commodity X. You don't care about it, because you don't need it, and you also can't imagine that you will ever need it. Suddenly you hear that Commodity X has become scarce. Demand is higher than supply and whoever wants to have the item has to ask around in many stores and wait for a long time or have good connections to get it. You still don't want Commodity X, but you become a little more interested in it. And then you hear that this item has suddenly been made illegal. It is bought and sold only in secret and, if people talk about it at all, they only do so in a whisper. Now, finally, you want to have Commodity X too. At first, you feel only a slight desire, but then your desire grows and grows. And, after a while, when Commodity X has been illegal for long enough, you believe that you cannot live without it, that you cannot live without an item which, some time ago, you were convinced you never needed.

That is half of the explanation why certain books have become so important in my country and, with them, literature in general. Here's the second half of the explanation: I live in a country that has only one single newspaper. To be sure, it has forty or fifty different names. It is not only called *Neues Deutschland*, the main newspaper of the Party, but also *Freies Volk* and *Tribüne* and *Die Leichtathletik*. Variations in name aside, it is still really only one single newspaper, because it has the same editor-in-chief. And this editor-in-chief is, at the same time, the head of programming for all the radio stations in the country and all the TV stations. On top of that, he executes his office in a very authoritarian and systematic way. What this means is that all these newspapers, journals, magazines and radio and television stations represent only one opinion, namely his, the editor-in-chief's.

As an almost inescapable result, books are the only public forum in the GDR where any kind of intellectual controversy is taking place, where disagreements are discussed, where different opinions meet and where everything is not yet organized into Above and Below and Left and Right. There is still curiosity when one reaches for a book, a curiosity that no longer exists when one opens a newspaper and that radio can only inspire when it plays music. As a consequence, literature in a country like mine has a function that is both unnecessary and impossible in a country like yours: It is at the same time a source of information and the site of intellectual controversies and also the only place where public dissatisfaction with some conditions can be voiced. At least sometimes. This is neither completely good nor completely bad.

As a result, the entertainment value of literary texts—and I am not using this phrase contemptuously —has naturally taken a back seat. It is clear, in my opinion, that these books have begun to carry more weight and this means, literally, that they have become heavier and often more heavy-handed. They are not written as carelessly as books here in the West sometimes are. However, with this lack of careless-ness, books also often lose their lightness. I am not saying that it happens in every single case, but I see a lot of cases like this and would therefore call it a tendency.

Whenever I have spoken of the resonance of liter-ature in the GDR so far, I have really only been talking about the resonance books find with the authorities. But, since authorities can develop pretty much anything except for good taste, they are never seriously interested in literature. Their concern is really only for certain parts of books and individual sentences. More plainly put, the only thing in my work that interests the Department of Cultural Affairs is its value for the politics of the day.

But even for real readers, for people who have to pay for books, literature means something other than it does here in the West. More clearly stated: I think that in the GDR, at least seven out of ten readers are people who work eight hours a day. This is, of course, not without relevance for the particular kind of interest these people have in literature. I'll throw some more statistics at you. When I do ten readings in West Germany, they are distributed approximately like this: I read five times at universities, three times at large bookstores in front of their core audiences, and twice at literary clubs or literary societies. I assume that both the kinds of readings and the number of readings would be very similar were I to tour Great Britain. But when I do ten readings in the GDR, the breakdown looks like this: I read three times at universities, once in a village in front of farmers, and six times in factories in front of workers and other employees. These numbers are certainly not mathematically correct because I haven't kept count, but they do represent the tendency of my observations. And I am absolutely sure those are correct.

The discussions and the conversations that are conducted after readings in the GDR most often differ significantly from those that I have experienced in the West. The most pronounced difference, I think, is that, in the GDR, the aesthetic aspects of the text I have read play only a minor part. It is much more important for the listeners to talk about the problems depicted and it is even more important for them to talk about their own. What I said earlier about books, that they are the only public place in the GDR where political disagreements are discussed, is true in a certain way for writers as well. They are expected to give different answers than the usual ones, different answers than the ones that are already known from the newspapers or the radio or assembly meetings. That means that one does not mainly want to be entertained by books, but rather one hopes for answers from them. One expects advice, life advice. That sounds like a very big word, and it is, but I still use it because I have had this experience over and over again.

Mind you, I am not talking about whether this is good or bad. I am not asking whether individual writers enjoy this situation or suffer in it. I am also not asking whether literature can fulfil this demand or whether it is immensely overstrained by it. And I am not asking whether a task falls on books that cannot be the task of books. I am only discussing my opinion about the situation of literature in the GDR. Literature must confront this situation and handle it, whether it wants to or not.

It is not at all my opinion that writers should do market research before they start writing a book, that is, that they should find out what as many readers as possible want to hear. That happens often in the East and in the West, and usually, when it happens, trivial literature emerges in both places. It is also not my opinion that literature should be permitted to ignore the needs of readers or pretend that these needs exist on a lower level and are unworthy of its attention. And, if I might be permitted such a sweeping generalization, this happens more often than not with Western literature. When I use the word literature here, I mean what is deemed 'great literature'. I think this is an important reason why literature in the West is mainly a matter for intellectuals and not a matter for farmers and workers and other employees. These people often feel abandoned by books and that's why they pick up things that might look like books but really aren't.

I am convinced that good and important books don't come into being when an author examines what problems people have and then thoroughly researches those problems and those people and then writes about it. That is how travel writing, which is really only writing about other people's concerns, comes into being but not important literature. I think good books only come into being when authors write about their own experiences, about their own misfortune or luck, their own doubts and discontents and hopes.

At best, writers' problems are the same or similar to those of other people. Most writers I know in the

GDR don't lead a life of seclusion deep in the forest or up in the ivory tower. Most live like most other people and, because of this, the resonance of their books is great. That's the whole secret and it's really no secret at all. It merely means that, for us, literature is nothing exclusive. It is not a luxury article but an everyday thing. And precisely that seems to be the reason why literature from the GDR meets with an increasingly wider response in the West, at least in West Germany, as well. It's not worth mentioning that a lot of banality is produced this way, definitely not less than in your country. The production of books is, after all, not just a question of the circumstances in which an author is living. It is also a question of his abilities. And that's truly a blessing.

I find this last fact particularly important. A vast majority of the writers in the GDR are living lives that are similar to the lives of a vast majority of their readers. And the vast majority of the writers in the GDR perceive themselves as socialists. Whether they would be socialists had they been living under different circumstances, that is, in another country or under a different balance of power, is a question I find metaphysical and irrelevant, at least in connection with the topic of our talk. I'll say it again: The vast majority of the writers in the GDR are socialists. Their political engagement affects the impact of their books and the impact of their books produces a large portion of their problems. The Party knows very well why it needs to keep a sharp eye on writers.

Most writers in the West don't associate them-selves with a particular political agenda. On the con-trary, it is considered narrow-minded and naive or hopelessly un-modern or even dogmatic to advocate any particular political programme. This kind of detachment when it comes to politics, I dare say, has led to the social ineffectiveness of literature. And this ineffectiveness results in the widespread liberality of writers in the West. In other words, the price writers in so-called Western democracies pay to be able to write, in principle, whatever they want is pretty high in my eyes. The price is that literature has no effect on anything and no impact except for producing a few reviews every now and then and sometimes stirring things up among insiders. Why in God's name should a society treat its literature restrictively when this lit-erature doesn't change anything anyway and is there-fore harmless? On the contrary, the criticism voiced in books is seen as an example of the liberality of Western society, but what is often overlooked is the fact that criticism isn't worth very much when it remains between the covers of a book.

I am aware, of course, that this is an exaggera-tion, that these observations are crude and that there are, of course, individual cases that disprove my the-ory. But I don't want to talk about that. They are, after all, only individual examples.

I have mentioned that, among you here in the West, an author can espouse his opinion in books without much interference. He only has one hurdle to jump: He has to find a publisher who thinks this opinion will sell. This is the only considerable form of censorship that takes place, the censorship of the free market. A book is, in many aspects, a commodity like any other and, whether the individual writer wants to or not, whether he is conscious of it or not, his book must conform to the laws of supply and demand. At least in principle.

This kind of censorship does not exist in countries like the GDR. Since the laws of the market have been suspended in all areas, they do not apply to books either. Instead, there is a form of ideological and political censorship. It is not called censorship, but that's what it is and it is very attentive. By the way, I consider ideological censorship, the kind that concerns itself with the changes a book brings about in its readers' heads, no more unethical than the censorship of the market. On the contrary, the only question is how this censorship is exercised, and, unfortunately, it is often carried out by lousy architects.

I don't want to hide the fact that I myself belong to the group of people who think that, in a socialist country, a certain kind of literary censorship makes sense. But this censorship must not follow the more or less arbitrary course of the current party line or comply with the necessities of the ever-changing politics of the day. It must rest on principles that are more reliable than those that are the result of snap judgements. Around 1950, Bertolt Brecht gave what I think is the most valid and most feasible answer to the question which kind of literature should be suppressed in a socialist country. Brecht maintained that all those writings should be censored that practice race-baiting, that glorify violence, propagate war or contain fascist propaganda. That I find okay. And that also means that every other literature should be published and made available to the public. But that is far from being the case in the GDR.

The path a manuscript has to travel from the writer to the press in our country is easy to describe. I give my manuscript to a publishing company just like other authors all over the world. Once I have come to an agreement with the publisher, they give my manuscript—and this does not happen all over the world—to a certain department in the Ministry of Culture. After reviewing the manuscript, this department grants a print permit, a kind of license, and then the book can be printed. That's all there is to it.

It must be said that the rejection of a manuscript by the Ministry of Culture is quite rare. In fact it is so rare that the number of rejected books can barely be expressed in percentages. That means that only very few books are actually banned in the GDR. Too many still, there is no question, and always in cases where Brecht's criteria do not apply. But still very few. That might be strange news to you, because you have most certainly heard of several such cases. And that is no coincidence. In the West, the best-known books from the East are the books that are not printed there. In the eyes of many Western publishers, a book from the GDR could have no greater virtue than being banned in the GDR. But cetainly not all books printed outside the GDR are good. And certainly not all books that are printed in the GDR are bad either.

The Western or Eastern preference for books that have problems with censorship derives, in my opinion, from cold war mentality. It makes the situation for the writers concerned complicated and unnecessarily difficult, since their literature is misused for something it doesn't want to be and should not be. Here, I am speaking from my own experience. My most recent book *Sleepless Days* has been banned in the GDR. It is a book by a socialist writer, written out of concern for the development of socialism in the GDR. It has appeared only in the West. Now, when many Western newspapers praise me for my book, it is certainly not out of concern for the development of socialism in the GDR. Rather, as I see it, the opposite is the case. The publicity granted here in the West to some writers who are banned in the East is not at all meant to initiate a discussion of their opinions or to

help further their cause. It is often only meant to
increase problems for the Eastern governments and to
demonstrate to the population in the West how unde-
mocratically things are done in socialist countries.
And, incidentally, the books are also supposed to sell.
I don't claim that these are the only reasons Western
publishers publish books banned in the East, but it is
quite often so. At least, I would say, most of the time.
Often, the help offered to the writer comes from a
very reactionary group, a camp with which he would
much rather not be affiliated. I myself, for example,
wish I could talk about my GDR-problems only with
people here in the West who are also interested in a
democratization of their own country.

I want to briefly mention another aspect of censorship without which this phenomenon's description
would be incomplete. I have said that only very few
books are banned in the GDR, and that is, without a
doubt, the truth. But what one really must consider is
just how many books never get written in the first
place. How many writers take the work off the censor's plate by inviting censorship into their own
heads, that is, by thinking about the difficulties of
censorship from the beginning and avoiding them, in
short, by becoming opportunists. Of course, I cannot
give you numbers—because what does not actually
happen cannot be captured by statistics. But I have
no doubt that there are many books that do not get

written. And that is a great loss for the literature of a country. And probably not just for its literature either.

A writer can't choose the circumstances of his life. He can, however, escape them. And when he chooses to, he often ends up paying the price by compromising his own identity. He can also bide his time and try to be comfortable in the situation. That happens often too and, again, the price the writer pays is his own identity. The result, which can be seen in the books of many writers, is surviving instead of actually living.

As a third possibility, the writer might try to gain control over the situation or at least some influence, because he realizes that this situation wasn't brought about by natural forces, but that it was produced by humans and is constantly being determined by interests. A writer who behaves like this, any person who behaves like this, behaves politically. And he will quickly realize that there is only one way he can gain influence over the situation around him: by daring to try and change it.

By making this statement, I do not want to claim that what makes a writer good is knowing exactly what is necessary and what isn't and being able to push for that in one's books. I do believe that a certain kind of ignorance, a 'non-knowledge' or 'non-understanding', just like a certain kind of ambition, motivates the creative human being to abolish it. It would make no sense at all to expect answers and answers only from books. In the East and in the West, what writers probably have in common is that they are seekers. Often, their literature is nothing but an attempt to find their way in the midst of the general sense of helplessness and to live in it.

Translated by Martin Bäumel and Tracy Graves

RESISTANCE IN *Jakob der Lügner*

In a letter Heinz Wetzel wrote months ago, he confronted me with the question why active resistance does not play any part in this book. Since resistance is so noticeably and consistently absent for no apparent reason, he doubted that I would be able to explain the omission.

To me the problem seems to be a central issue in the book; and because to write or not to write about resistance in this context was a moral decision (though by no means *only* a moral decision) which touches upon the very foundation of the book, I want to speak about this theme above everything else. Heinz Wetzel's presumption that I would have no reasons to give for the absence of resistance in this story is not exactly right. On the contrary, I have so many reasons that I don't even know which one I should begin with.

But first I would like to say a word about our different situations.

You are all ornithologists and I am a bird. It is known that a constellation such as this can—and perhaps even must—present communication problems. It is also known that ornithologists try to understand the language of birds, but not vice versa. The birds indeed are normally a little bit better at chirping and a little better at flying—but that's a different story. At any rate, I've never heard of a nightingale in a zoo being promoted to the director of an aviary. In a word—I absolutely don't consider *you* incompetent to speak about the question which we have under discussion—rather myself. You will hear my own views about my book—views that by no means have to be the established truth. They may be random or shallow or even both. And I even think it's probable that after our discussion I will know more about a book of mine than I know now. But I do not think it is probable that the book would have been better if I had known all that beforehand. Such is my confused relationship to literary criticism.

Now about resistance: I'm sure I don't have to tell you here the extent to which the Jews were persecuted during the last war. The facts are known and for the last thirty-eight years mankind has had to live with these facts. It has done so quite well. Ever since I have been able to think, I have been preoccupied with the

question why the resistance against Jewish extermina-
tion—I mean the Jewish resistance, the resistance of
the victims—was so unbelievably small. This is not
the right occasion to analyse the possible reasons.
Here I would only like to say a few words about the
extent of this resistance.

The whole of Eastern Europe was covered with
ghettos. The ghettos were the waiting rooms to the
concentration camps where millions of people—
whether aware or unaware of it—awaited their exter-
mination. I was put into one of these ghettos as a
small child. If I'm not mistaken it was the largest one
there was, in Łódź. And now listen: There is only one
single case known where Jews pulled together to
defend themselves against their persecutors. It was the
Warsaw Ghetto Uprising which Heinz Wetzel used as
an example in his letter. Here and there there were
what perhaps could be called small flareups. But these
don't deserve the name 'organized resistance' and, by
the way, they never took place in the concentration
camps. That is all. In those hundreds of ghettos people awaited their end silently. Perhaps hopeful of
some miracle of liberation, perhaps too weak to
defend themselves or too afraid, or perhaps too dis-
couraged. Nowhere, except in this one case, was the
fist pulled out of the pocket.

Is it appropriate to cite the Warsaw Ghetto
Uprising as an example, as if it were at the beginning

of a list? I don't think so. This instance was unprecedented and unique. It was more a big exception than an example. If a writer portrays resistance from this period, and doesn't use the Warsaw Ghetto as an illustration, this has to trigger the question in the perceptive reader: Where could it have been? Naturally, an author is able to ignore this question, and it is possible that I would have, had there not been other considerations.

I ask all of you—after this short and probably unnecessary historical oration—to ask yourselves the question what has become of resistance in the literature about this period. Without exaggerating you can say that in books it has made an astonishing career. Without exaggerating you can surely say that the literature about this period is really literature about the resistance. The big exception has suddenly become the rule—the unheard-of and unique became an every-day occurrence. The reasons are obvious. It is more pleasing to believe that victims defend themselves; it is more pleasing to believe that injustice has a hard time succeeding; it is more pleasing to believe that the number of resistance fighters was large. With the years this number has continually grown. Just like the number of those who were fascists with the years decreases. Come today to Germany and listen around—you would think that Hitler stood alone in the pasture.

This is what I'm leading up to—how the role of resistance in literature has become inflated, and how this subsequently lessened the feats of those who actually did put up a resistance. They were the big heroes, the big exceptions; the abundance of resistance in books however makes them commonplace. And the others: the unheroic, those who were afraid, who were apathetic, the insignificant, the cowards, thus almost all—they somehow get lost in the books, they hardly exist.

I would like to say a few words about the way in which the idea for this book came into my head. One day my father said to me that he had known a man in the ghetto—a hero that I absolutely have to write about. What's so special about him, I asked. This man, my father went on to say, had kept a radio hidden in the ghetto. This was forbidden on penalty of death. He secretly heard foreign stations: Radio London, Radio Moscow—and the ghetto inhabitants who were totally cut off from the outside world were provided with news. One day this was betrayed to the Germans, by a spy or out of carelessness. The man was arrested and a short time later he was shot. He had been a big hero said my father with tears in his eyes, and it really would be worthwhile to write about him. I also found this man to be a hero, but I didn't have the slightest desire to write about him. Because I had often read about this man—thousands of books had already been written about him. Strictly speaking almost every book that I had read about the fascist era was about this very man. Over the years I forgot the story until it once again came to my mind, only with the difference which you already know.

I have come to another point I want to speak about. It was never my intention to portray a historical picture; neither in this book nor in any other. I never intended to give the reader a kind of historical lecture. At the same time I didn't want to distort the historical picture, though it was my intention to tell a decent story. As I gathered together the materials for it, I had to answer for myself the question what the prerequisites of my story would be. I want to name two. One of them was this: that most readers had heard too much of the little amount of resistance there had been. Another consisted in the fact that in this story there was no place for resistance. Such as I saw it, resistance had no business there. It would only have disturbed me in my concentration, in a tranquility that (as I found at the time) this story very much needed.

I don't want to explain this story to you. You are more predestined for that than I am. I only want to say that its motives do not lie in the past. I presume that any decent book needs a motive which comes from the time when it is written. This motive should not be allowed to consist solely in the desire to tell a story. For example, I had the desire to meditate upon the question of what role hope plays in the lives of people. Whether it is sufficient for survival, or whether it is only helpful when it spurs people into action. For example, into resisting.

I was also preoccupied with the question whether lying is a purely cognitive theoretical category or whether it also has a moral dimension. I wanted to know if there is a level at which the rules of logic become unimportant and obsolete and are replaced by the rules of morality.

What I also wanted (although I'm probably not saying anything new) was to write a story about the value of storytelling, above all in times of misery; whether it can help people to survive, or distract them from the worries they would have been better off taking care of. And then I ask you—what does resistance have to do with all this? In particular a resistance which has already got far too much publicity when you look at its minimal size.

To close, I have one more thing to say which will spoil everything; with which I will probably destroy the small impression that my arguments may have made on one or another of you. But I'm going to have to say it anyway—because it also belongs here. The only theme in this book, so it seems to me, is resistance.

'Culture' is probably one of the most diversely and most frequently defined terms. I do not want to add to the vast spectrum of definitions, many of which, I feel fortunate, I do not know. As I recently read, they range from 'the entirety of the material and spiritual conditions of life' to 'the state of the collective soul'. I find something plausible in almost each one and it probably depends on my own state of mind as to which one I find most convincing at any given moment. For now, all I want to do is state that, for my purposes, 'Culture' appears to me to be sufficiently defined if one views it as a kind of orientation point in the sky or as a kind of enterprise that is supposed to protect us from 'Un-Culture', as varied as our images of that might be. When people speak about 'Culture', they are of course speaking about their own, but points of contact with the ideas of others, within their own political camp and outside of it, are unavoidable. These points of contact are what we should talk about. Nevertheless, when I use the term 'Culture' in the following pages as if it needs no explanation, please always hear it in quotes as a sign of the imprecision and dubiousness that always accompany it.

I think that the cultural standard within a society essentially depends on two factors: the self-confidence of its members and their faith in the future. To act and live culturally implies believing that one's way of life and behaviour are fairly important. Furthermore, it implies that one believes that this way of life and behaviour are worth preserving. And that one believes in the possibility of preservation itself.

But wherever you look, people live in the aware-ness of their impotence. They feel that they are excluded from the most important decisions in the Eastern and the Western world; they feel that they don't matter. No one cares if they approve and their disapproval carries no weight. Their governments treat them with increasing brazenness, allegedly for their own good. People are constantly insecure, in a state of permanent anxiety, so that for most of them 'Accommodate Yourself' and 'Conceal Your Doubt' have become the normal forms of existence. Of course, almost none of this is happening under its real name. In the relationship between a government and its citizens, it is taken for granted that things are characterized as their opposites: Spiritual incapacitation is called free development, an intimidated nod is tantamount to free expression, bigotry bears the name of free will, indoctrination is commensurate with the free formation of opinion and obedience is equivalent to volunteering.

I don't think it is a coincidence that many aspects of the decline of culture are especially visible in the two countries where these principles are put into practice most consistently and most successfully, that is, in the United States and the Soviet Union. I am not disregarding the top-quality products of high-   performance artists that, without a doubt, do exist. I am speaking of a way of dealing with one another, which is where culture expresses itself first and foremost: people with people, authorities and countries with citizens, and countries with other countries. And I am speaking of their influence on the rest of the world, an influence that grows larger and larger and becomes particularly devastating where satellite states feel the need to demonstrate submissiveness. A submissiveness, by the way, for which the term 'alliance loyalty'[1] has been invented.

One important, not necessary, but at least possible and probable, consequence of self-confidence is tolerance. Yet the inevitable consequence of a lack of self-confidence is intolerance. This holds true, it seems to me, for individuals as well as for groups or even for

society. Wherever self-confidence is the least pronounced, the *others* will have the most difficulties.
They might be critics, protesters, foreigners, Jews, quite
simply *others*. Of course, there can also be economic
interests behind such resentments. In my opinion, however, it is intolerance that opens the gates of hostility
and brings a kind of hatred to the fore of which people
with self-confidence are simply not capable.

We live in societies that owe a large part of their
coherence to the concept of enemies. In the GDR, for
example, the Unites States is seen mainly as a mono-
capitalist, imperialist country, and the publicly available news about America is largely about things that
support this point of view. Now, the USA is indeed a
mono-capitalist, imperialist country. But it also has
many other facets. These other facets should not be
concealed from the public, even though they might
destroy the public's image of the USA as an enemy.
The reverse story: In 1978, I spent some time in the
USA and read the *New York Times* every day for
about half a year. During this time, I found two
reports on the GDR. First, a young man managed to
escape the country in the trunk of a Belgian diplo-
mat's car. Second, a Russian soldier went on a shoot-
ing spree at the intersection of Unter den Linden and
Friedrichstraße. The End.

Producing images of one's enemies, accepting
them and subsequently relying on their accuracy, all

this generates a constant hostility toward culture. Naturally, intolerance spreads in this environment. It appears to be a vital precaution. There is a certain amount of violence without which, it is said, we would be at the enemy's mercy little by little. In reality, this violence hinders the people themselves more than it does the enemy. It makes their lives more miserable than any enemy ever could. Its consequence is an atmosphere of suspicion and spying, an atmosphere where nothing counts more than the proof of loyalty, where lip service is in great demand, where people are asked to gradually replace their judgement with prejudice.

The persecution of 'degenerates' is one example, whether of 'degenerate art' or 'degenerate people'. Or a slogan from the same period in history, which seems comparatively harmless: 'Shh, the enemy is listening!' The McCarthy committees on Un-American Activities are an example. Closer to home, there is the decree against radicals in civil service and the ensuing employment bans. The ubiquity of the State Security Services in the lives of GDR citizens is another example. Once you begin to list them, it is difficult to stop.

As I see it, the problem lies in the fact that most people find the examples from the history and camp of the opposing political system much more plausible than those more immediate to them. This insensitivity itself is an example. It demonstrates how dealing with images of the enemy has become a matter of course. This view of the world has a destructive effect on culture in various ways. It not only promotes acceptance of intolerance and violence in one's own country, it also prevents us from seeing the cultural achievements of the *others*. The *other* culture is missing, so one contents oneself with a half—one's own. One refuses to see the other culture. I don't want to start another catalogue. I simply want to say that it would do both camps a lot of good to learn about the cultural achievements of the other side. And they should hurry up, because these achievements are decreasing on a daily basis.

We probably agree that a society's cultural standards must not be confused with its material wealth. If that were the case, if there were necessary connections, we would have a great yardstick by which to measure culture: the gross national product or the per capita use of energy or artificial fertilizer. And it would be obvious who is in the top bracket. But our relationship to commodities and their quickest and most comprehensive annihilation cannot be a substitute for the attitudes and convictions that are the precondition of culture. Nevertheless, many people believe that this is the case. Actually, most do. In Western industrialized societies, it is considered a fact that progress and growth are inextricably linked to one another. In other words, it is possible to declare the goals of industry and commerce to be the goals of the general public. And in the Eastern states, under 'real existing socialism', the same notion has gained acceptance, albeit at a lower level of production. There, growing consumption is the main goal. It becomes the measure of progress as well, because the governing parties deem this goal to be more easily achievable and probably more desirable than the realization of the grand intentions with which they came to power: to revolutionize the relationship of people to one another. That is a mistake in two respects, maybe one of the most horrible and most far-reaching mistakes of our time.

Now, let's talk about the second factor responsible for the cultural decline in our time: the lack of confidence, the growing certainty that a future is barely obtainable and, if it is, then it won't hold anything good in store.

More and more, people live in a state of panic. They are surrounded by threats that loom larger every day. Never mind the fact that these threats have been known for a long time and could theoretically be overcome. The fear of war is spreading, the fear of ecological collapse, the fear of unemployment (and, therefore, of poverty), the fear of radioactivity, to mention just a few, and only those from so-called affluent countries.

Those that loudly and publicly recommend optimism, mostly politicians, military officers and businessmen, preach a wrong kind of confidence. Confidently, they want to continue on as usual and for that they desire calm and order. They want to continue doing with confidence what has cost millions of people all confidence. Whoever rebels against this inevitably begins to inhabit the uncomfortable and often existence-threatening role of the outsider, no matter where he lives. The government of the Federal Republic of Germany maintains that the protests of the peace movement are 'controlled by Communists'. The government of the GDR describes the participants of the peace movement as 'tools of Western principals' and treats them accordingly. Both reactions follow their own logic, both are horribly similar, both are a good reason to add another considerable fear to the ones that already exist. And that is how calm and order reign, by force, which is, to me, the most visible sign of the cultural decline in our time.

I have been dealing with the question as to whether there is a need, a conviction or characteristic that could be seen as the foundation of a 'culture-filled' existence. Probably not. The closest concept, in my opinion, is solidarity. Solidarity implies an interest that goes beyond one's own person and one's own existence. It has to do with responsibility, with sympathy, with self-love as much as with selflessness. It carries more culture in its wake than, for example, the love of art or the promotion of the sciences or the cultivation of traditions. That is not to say that the love of art, the promotion of the sciences and the cultivation of traditions could stand in the way of a flourishing culture. It is quite simply that one encounters them too often in places where there is no trace of faith in the future, no evidence of confidence.

Of course, there is a kind of solidarity that should not exist. One can team up in support of a wretched cause and act in solidarity in its favour. Which kind of solidarity is the right kind cannot be decided in general terms and that's not what it is about either. Here, I want to point out that solidarity is oriented toward the future; it is optimistic. At the same time, such solidarity is evidence of self-confidence: Why would you stand up for something if you are convinced of your own weakness? And that is exactly why states, institutions, authorities in both parts of our world interfere with solidarity wherever they encounter it. They want their people to be isolated, in competition with one another, under control and submissive. The need for solidarity, which is probably not dead, is satisfied by the call for a kind of solidarity that inconveniences the other side. Here, for example, solidarity with the interned in Poland, with occupied Afghanistan. There, for example, solidarity with Nicaragua or the victims of Israeli aggression. Not that I consider such kinds of solidarity inappropriate or superfluous. But it is imperative that one sees the side effects of their public propagation, that is, the use of solidarity in the production of images of the enemy. This kind of solidarity is promoted when people don't act with one another based on their own concerns and when they don't counteract immediate threats. Once they do act in solidarity with one another, retribution pours in from all sides. They are soon treated like agents of the enemy. However differently, they are made to endure the struggle for survival and this can easily make cultural needs seem like a luxury.

So, what to do?

It would be very naive to give any advice here. Luckily, I am not tempted, since I don't have any. All I can do is prescribe the course of action that seems best to me. More attention should be paid to violence in our relationships, be it violence in the relationship of one person to another, or violence that a government inflicts on its people, or one that countries inflict on other countries. We should pay closer attention to this violence and react more strongly against it. We should despise it more than we do today. People should stop taking for granted that the representation of their interests is in the right hands. They should begin to feel responsible for themselves. The great cultural achievements of our time would be disarmament, elimination of hunger in more than half of the world, care for our environment. We have to wish that more and more people will realize their responsibility in all of this. It is a miserably long road from the consciousness of one's own impotence to the consciousness of one's strength. But, if we want to have any kind of future, there is no other way.

Translated by Martin Bäumel and Tracy Graves

Note

1 The German word 'Bündnistreue' implies an unquestioned loyalty to the larger political or social entity of which one is a part.

Although I do not regard our so-called civil rights as a supreme accomplishment, as a goal after which there is nothing to be achieved or to wish for, they still represent an invaluable good—a virtue that must be preserved, that deserves to be defended, that must not be put at the disposal of allegedly higher interests. Despite this and without a doubt, you as well as I, at least for the moment, are living in a country in which these rights are facing hard times. There are recognizable efforts to introduce a kind of permanent emergency law, which—however critically one might evaluate the history of the Federal Republic of Germany—would be a major turning point. It seems to me that this process is not just looming as a threatening possibility, a dark foreshadowing which, with a bit or even a lot of luck, is not certain to come true, but that it is fully under way. And, if there are not enough people who resist it (thereby making use of a fundamental right which is more and more in disrepute), we will reach this 'turning point' soon.

Some of you may already be aware that I come from the GDR and, due to a number of circumstances, the explanation of which I will spare you on this occasion, I am suddenly standing here in front of you. I only mention this in response to a criticism that has not been brought forward by any of you so far, but which I am sure to face later on; it has always been quick to come. Whenever I speak about those conditions in West Germany that appear worth criticizing to me (and there are many), the immediate response is always: So, how is that in the GDR, why don't you talk about that? Or, as soon as I say a word about the military regime in Turkey, someone shouts: And what about Poland? And if I dare to say the words Nicaragua and CIA in the same breath, I hear: So you forgot all about Afghanistan then? And as soon as I openly express my fears about Pershings and cruise missiles, someone suggests to me that I should be much more afraid of the SS 20. Constantly someone is missing a certain proportionality in my remarks, a kind of balance that I see myself unfit for. I am a bit calmed by the thought that this balance exists because of the many people in this country, who stand for the exact opposite, who do not have even the slightest balance and are not quite without influence.

Nevertheless, I do not mind meeting these demands, which are expressed so fiercely and so often. Before I begin, I would like to state that many of the local grievances are to be found to the same or an even greater extent in the GDR. Now, don't let this declaration pacify you. You should not belong to those who think that an injustice becomes somehow more bearable because the same injustice exists somewhere else.

The extent to which the rights of the citizen are respected in a society is largely determined by the objectives and ideals of that society. By that I do not mean the verbally communicated objectives but the real ones, because constitutions contain a lot of things. If you look at reality, the basic principle that no one should be discriminated against because of their political views, for example, must appear to you as pure mockery. Of course this principle is not missing from any constitution. Imagine an article in the constitution that states: Whoever represents the views favoured by the government, even if they are not his own, will be treated preferentially. Outrageous!, everyone would shout, what kind of a state makes these kind of rules! In practice, however, this rule is of iron validity. And the question is what should be considered more depressing: Whether such a directive is put down on paper or is simply in effect.

Not too long ago, I was invited to a school, to a discussion with seventeen and eighteen-year-old students. For a while it went well. Of course we talked about the GDR, the role of literature there, the censorship. They wanted to know from me, how censorship works if you are exposed to it, what its effects are. To be honest, I was not very comfortable with this kind of interest, because I do not believe that students, who have very little accurate and generally prejudiced information about the GDR anyway, should be taught first and foremost about the censorship there. Nevertheless, the interest was there and, after all, I was standing in front of the class as a principal witness of sorts (this was probably the main reason I was invited), so I made an effort to live up to their expectations and not beat around the bush. At one point I said, the most significant result of censorship is probably not the fact that four or five books are banned every year, however unjustified the grounds may be, but the fact that a hundred more books are not even written. The class accepted this information approvingly; they had not expected anything else from me. Later, when we got to the topic of the Federal Republic, the levels of consensus shrunk. The young people, most of whom were planning to become dentists, shareholders or pharmacists, reacted angrily to my criticism. On the one hand, it appeared to them to be exaggerated and, on the other hand, they felt that someone like me was not entitled to such criticism and that I had retroactively cancelled out my reproach of the conditions in the GDR. Soon I was of the impression that I was facing a cohesive group of young reactionaries. I do not wish to conceal that I was appalled and reacted in a more intense and emotional way than I might have otherwise. The only person who fully agreed with me, it seemed, was their teacher.

Later, as he accompanied me on my way out, he amicably patted me on the back and said that it had been a long time since the school last heard opinions of this kind. I told him that his consent would have filled me with even more joy and would have been more helpful, if he had expressed it earlier during my scuffle with the students. He smiled softly and gave me a short lecture about the situation at the school, about the situation of trainee teachers, about the situation on the labour market. He also said a few words about the *Radikalenerlass*.[1] In the end I had no choice but to come to a conclusion that was similar to the one I had argued in front of the students. The actual purpose of the *Radikalenerlass* was not the suspension of a couple of teachers and a couple of civil servants every year. The more important consequence was that tens of thousands of people were scared of it and kept their mouths shut. The suspensions were, at most, a side effect and probably an undesired one: They end up being embarrassing, there is clamour, and there are always troublemakers who want to take it to court. The inventors of the ordinance would prefer it if suspensions were the exception and fear was the rule in exactly the same way the censors dream of not having to ban any more books because they are all filled with authorized trains of thought.

The state, every state, is an ominous structure. Although allegedly one if its primary duties is to serve the interests of the majority of its citizens and to protect their rights, it does develop a self-interest which is not immediately recognizable. Suddenly civil rights contradict the state's interest and must, therefore, be restricted. The most varied constitutions seem to agree that the state should be the subject of continuous suspicion, an object of close monitoring and that the permanent control of the state by its citizens is inextricably linked to the essence of every democracy. In theory there is definitely a consensus on this question. In reality, however, the relationship is reversed: The one who is supposed to be controlled becomes the controller. The state does not trust its citizens, it wants to register and supervise and regulate and keep track of things. Calls for the state's containment are dismissed as subversive and, according to its own concept of itself, they are. Observations and experiences of this kind are easy to make in any part of the world, for example in the East and West. Neither side should be all too proud of this similarity.

The coherence of a society partly arises from the fact that its members, however different their interests may be, feel a common threat from the outside and share a desire for protection from this threat. It appears to me that the fear of Communism is a central connector within West German society, if not the main one. Without the common enemy, I claim, the discrepancies in this society would be more evident. Those who have an interest in preserving the current state of affairs, let's call them politely the conservatives, are therefore keen not to let this common enemy fade out of the picture. So, they paint enemy's image with fresh colours every day and they report about his dangerousness and disreputability daily with staggering success. Whenever forced to live in danger, people must move closer together and limit themselves. That is clear. One cannot pedantically insist on every right when there is so much at stake. So we are driven to cede our authority, which we would rather have kept for ourselves. And we have to put up with things that are rather unpleasant to us. Life in fear and insecurity produces opportunists. I do not think of opportunism as a sign of a weak character. Where fitting in has become a mass phenomenon, like in the Federal Republic or the GDR, there have to be societal reasons for it. In both places, conformity is rewarded while non-conformity (in children we call it originality) is punished. We already live in a country in which trust in authority has a long tradition, in which inconspicuousness is seen as a great virtue and in which for many people 'well-behaved' and 'obedient' are synonyms.

Some of you may recall, how the Federal Republic reacted when the powerful protests against the deployment of Pershing II and cruise missiles began. Instantly, the chancellor and his ministers unanimously declared: In our country, these kinds of decisions are not made in the streets. Do you feel like I do about this, do you feel the arrogance behind this attitude? Do you also sense the underlying wish, that people would just cast their vote every four years and shut up for the rest of the time? People should not get involved in matters they do not know anything about. If their opinion is desired, they certainly will be asked.

When I say this, I do not mean that the government is obliged to take up any cause that people protest for. All I am talking about is an authoritarian attitude and the disregard shown for a fundamental right. Why else should the constitution consider the right to protest one of the inalienable basic rights, if not to inform the government about the desires of the masses, desires it should include in its decision-making? If the exertion of a right has no effect, that right becomes useless. At most it has the function of a safety valve, it is cosmetic, it has to do with hypocrisy and it lets the political circumstances appear more favourable than they actually are. In this instance, and I am talking about the protest against the deployment of missiles here, there is another point that should give the government something to think about, should it actually take the whole basic rights business seriously. What does it mean, when millions of people decide to protest, in a country where it is unusual for anyone to speak up, where people are used to acquiescing and putting up with things.

It seems remarkable to me that, while the federal government insists in this case on the authority it has over its population, when faced with the force planning to station the missiles, it concedes all authority and bows to American wishes in a way, which might well be called submissive. It is understandable that the Reagan and Weinberger administration, considering the fact that they assume an armed conflict between the East and West to be a possibility, have an interest in the majority of it taking place in Europe. It is even understandable why it would be convenient for the French government, if the stage for this possible confrontation were Germany rather than France. Why, however, the German government should agree with all this and not even slightly deviate from the views of those who plan to bring in the missiles at any cost cannot be explained with the concept of 'alliance loyalty'. Rather, it is linked to a concept of the enemy, to ideology, meaning the aforementioned anti-Communism, and not least of all with the fact that American interests, be they economic, military or imperial, are held by this government to be a kind of supreme commandment. It also applies here. The fact that Soviet interests are not quite absent from the GDR government's policies does not make things any better.

A right can be eroded, if those to whom it is granted lose the possibility, the courage or the ability to exercise it. The right to freedom of opinion, for example, can be threatened in various ways. On the one hand, we have the case of the TV journalist Franz Alt.[2] As you know, he is no longer allowed to present programmes that deal with the peace movement or armament resolutions because he has certain opinions on those topics, which he refuses to conceal. As they say, he lacks balance. The opposite lack of balance, however, has never bothered any of the officials. You can watch and listen to hundreds of programmes, none of which are fair or balanced. This imbalance in the media is demonstrated in every aspect from the phrasing of news broadcasts to derogatory remarks about peace activists made by a presenter of the *Sportschau*.[3] The honest accusation against Franz Alt should be that he is not one-sided in the desired way.

The right to freedom of opinion, to stick with the example, is also of little use to those who are conscious of their own powerlessness. He who has often enough experienced that all important decisions are made well above his head, that he does not and never will make a difference, that his opinion is of little interest to anyone, he will remain silent. Why get

agitated, why get involved, is his sad principle, if it
has no effect. Why speak up, if nobody cares? He will
teach his children that, while talking may be silver,
silence is golden. He sees the demonstrations on television, whose goals are actually much to his liking,
and shakes his head about the protesters, who refuse
to accept what he has known for a long time. Time
and again reality appears to prove him right.

At last, the right to freedom of opinion becomes
vacuous when millions of people simply do not have
an opinion, when they stop caring about public
affairs. This appears to me to be the case in the
Federal Republic. They live in a world of surrogate
concerns, taken there by glossy magazines, TV shows,
advertising, by a certain atmosphere. They make pay-
ments, buy, consume, throw out, buy again. It
demands all their attention. And they are calmed by
the thought that the important decisions of the nation
are in safe hands. Those, who are of a different opinion, are viewed as know-it-alls or even as subversives.
Some politicians, primarily those from the right end
of the political spectrum, call them the silent majority
and use them as an argument whenever resistance
crops up against their own politics. This always
meant sympathetically. 'Silent Majority' means:
Those people who are diligent, who go to work
instead of protesting, those who do not interfere in
things they do not know about. It becomes clear that

those politicians wish for a people that lives in a constant state of civic apathy. There is not much cost in granting all sorts of rights, as long as there is no danger of them being exercised.

I consider those circumstances desirable in which there is no silent majority, in which the majority is used to expressing their opinion and to taking part in public affairs. The precondition for this appears to be that the processes in a society are not viewed as mysterious and fundamentally immutable things, but rather as being determined by interests and susceptible to change. Citizens who insist on their rights—and those are the ones to wish for—must be politically interested citizens. This quality is not part of every citizen's chromosome set. It must be taught to them. But wherever teachers, who are at the least slightly critical of the present conditions, attempt to do so, the state shouts in an instant that this is a case of indoctrination and threatens severe consequences. Children and adolescents, it is said, must be given the opportunity to form their own opinions without being influenced by those of their teachers. As if there weren't any other influences! What presents itself as a demand for impartiality in education is, in reality, a massive attempt to produce apolitical citizens, that very silent majority.

No one is spared from developing some sort of relationship to the threats that those living today are exposed to. When faced with those threats, many people close their eyes and try to push them aside. This is a kind of relationship too. They build a wall between the outside world and their private existence and occasionally it works. If some alarming news gets through to them, they calm themselves with the thought that luckily there are professionals who will most likely take care of these problems. They are oblivious to the fact that those very professionals are the ones who created most of the problems in the first place. The politically immature aspect of such an existence does not reach their consciousness.

Then there are those who do recognize the dangers we are exposed to, but who deem resistance futile. They feel too powerless, disaster seems unavoidable to them. They live in desperation.

And finally there are people who see the dangers and who fight them. They are convinced that disasters that are started by people can also be averted by people. These people exercise their most important right: feeling responsible for oneself. They search for allies, they join forces and they put up resistance. Their behaviour is political and, at the same time, optimistic. To them not everything is lost, because they believe in their own power.

Translated by Jonathan Becker

Notes

1 The German ordinance that requires teachers and civil servants not to express anti-constitutional opinions.

2 Franz Alt was the moderator and producer of *Report Baden-Baden*, one of the most popular political news shows on West German television. He worked in these capacities for the show, now renamed *Report Mainz*, from 1972 to 1992.

3 A popular German sports news programme.

THIS IS UNRELIABLE INFORMATION

Marianna D. Birnbaum, University of California,
in conversation with Jurek Becker

MARIANNA D. BIRNBAUM: *Do you have good childhood memories?*

JUREK BECKER: Are there such things as good childhood memories? Up to what age do you consider a memory a childhood one?

Well, up to about ten.

No, I really don't have any good childhood memories.

No memories at all, or just no good ones?

I have very few memories altogether, and among them there are very few good ones.

Do you remember your mother?

No, I don't. I can see some dark pictures and movement, but when I try to identify them, they dissolve. It's not really a clearly drawn picture—she always has a different face. How she looks or behaves depends on my mood at the time, so it's not a reliable memory. I think that my mother is a theory for me—something I constructed out of a few bits of information my father gave me. There aren't any pictures or photographs of her.

Where do the various mother figures in your novels come from?

A while ago someone said that the characters in my novels only have fathers, and no mothers. This criticism is not entirely unfair, since the precisely created or, shall we say, epic figures are really mostly fathers; the mothers are just hinted at. . . . If I remember correctly, only one of my so-called main characters has a mother who is important for the plot. The 'I' in *Aller Welt Freund*[1] has a mother, Sonya; however, she's more like a sister than a mother. She's a mock-mother.

Some mothers are like that.

Some are, of course, that's why I dared to describe her that way. I only want to say that my 'mother-experiences' are very, very shallow. But one doesn't expect that an author can describe only what he's experienced; I rather like it when authors try to go beyond their own experiences. At any rate, my experiences with mothers are very limited and, surprisingly, so is my desire to describe them. However, that has nothing to do with my desire to describe women.

*But the relationships are different. Actually, there is
another mother in* Irreführung,[2] *who is an archetype,
'the Good German Mother'.*

Then it must be a cliché which I took over without thinking about it. Perhaps I wanted to describe
this mother to round the whole thing out. But I want
to say one thing from the start; you're asking me
about books which you may have read the day before
yesterday, and I'm answering about books I wrote fifteen years ago. Do you think I can pull all my motivations out of a hat and lay them immediately on the
table? Although I haven't become senile yet, I've just
simply forgotten quite a bit.

*Of course—I'll try to keep that in mind. May I ask,
what was the profession of your father?*

He worked in a textile factory which belonged to his
uncle; he was thus in quite a good position. He
belonged to the 'clan' of this factory, and ended up
working as a Prokurist[3]—what's called a *kaufmän-
nischer Angestellter*[4] in German bureaucratese.

*You portray yourself as a son quite often. Do you
have any self-portraits as a father? You're also a
father, aren't you?*

I really don't have any. It's always seemed like I've
fallen into this role by accident, by mistake.

You mean, into your role as father?

Yes. You know, there are situations in which I have to do something, and meanwhile I have the feeling that I'm totally insecure. Whenever I've been forced to talk and behave like a father, it's always seemed that I'm acting like a con-man. I've never thought that I had even a minimum of the qualifications to be a father.

Maybe like Kilian's mother.[5]

Perhaps. Maybe that's really a complex and suppressed self-portrait.

This is actually a side-question, but attempted suicide in your novels always involves gas. Why?

You make it sound like my books are swarming with suicides.

Not really—but Kilian in Aller Welt Freund *and Oswald in* Der Boxer.[6]

I swear, I've never thought of that before. It's an accident—or maybe it has something to do with mental laziness; perhaps I didn't want to make the effort. When I read about suicides in newspapers, they usually involve gas or sleeping pills. Since I've always had trouble with pills, but I have to deal with gas daily, this is perhaps the simpler solution. In other words, if I had to kill myself, I would definitely do it with gas.

Really?

Yes, even if you think it's surprising. How would you do it?

To me gas seems like a very effeminate way to commit suicide.

Are you disappointed that I wouldn't plunge a knife into my chest?

No, not at all. But you could hang yourself, or jump out a window; of course, that's not aesthetic. But still . . . I don't know; pills are the most usual way. Well, unlike Mark [in Der Boxer], you left the GDR only after the death of your father. Was this decision mainly a political one?

No, it wasn't. As. you know, I wasn't just taken and shown the door. I had good cause to be aggravated at the GDR; but where is it said that you can't be aggravated at the place where you live? I'm also aggravated at the place where I live now, in the West. One of the problems was that they didn't publish me in the GDR, and I wanted to live where I could be published. In addition, I was exposed to quite outrageous pressures, which were meant to intimidate me. In this situation, the fact that I'm choleric by nature helped me. The presence of a writer in his own country is probably not entirely without meaning. I hope that this doesn't sound too immodest. But what does the presence of a writer mean? Surely his physical presence must mean less than the presence of his text. My physical presence is only interesting for those four or five people which I happen to know; the rest have nothing from me. At that time, I was ready to add my physical presence to the presence of my text; but to sit around mutely seemed quite meaningless. That's the political background of the whole thing; but there was a second reason, and you could perhaps call it a private, or rather a work-related one. In 1977–78, I was involved in heavy political debate which was not only very excited, but also very exciting. When I look at the texts I wrote during that period, they don't represent what in my own mind I would call good literature. I don't like them. To put it differently, I don't believe that a barricade is a good place to formulate sentences. It is a place to compose manifestos, a place for rhetoric, but not for literature. Consciously or subconsciously, I was eager to remove everything private from my texts; I envisioned myself as being in a permanent battle which had many spectators, and I didn't want those spectators to arrive at the idea that I was weakening or giving up. This is a very unpleasant situation for an author, and, above all, a very unproductive one. It seemed to me as though I had to choose between two different careers: either to become a resistance-fighter or to remain a writer.

I know that many confuse the two, but they are not the same; there are some differences. As you know, I decided in favour of the one career at the expense of the other, and that's the second reason for my moving to the West, which still seems provisional today, even if it's of suspicious length.

Sometimes I'm asked whether my writing has changed. I'm sure it has; I'm quite sure that a writer's surroundings must have some effect on his way of writing. In the mean time, I've been printed again in the GDR; but I can't rid myself of the fear that, if I were to return tomorrow, I would write once more in a way which is not accepted there, and the whole circus would begin again. The fact that they publish me in the GDR has very little to do with changes in the GDR, but rather with changes in me. I would be afraid of conflicts of the old type; I don't mean a fear that there would be possible bureaucratic consequences, but rather that I would become indifferent. The idea is, 'My God, do I need that? Do I have time for that? Is it worth it?' This 'Is it worth it?' is a very important question. If I had a reason to believe that it was indeed worth it, I would possibly have the courage to move back to the GDR. However, my experiences tell me that I wouldn't change the GDR, only my own position. I no longer think that such struggles make much sense.

And you've put them behind you. As Thomas Mann said, 'Where I am, there German literature is.' But where are you at home? Do you feel comfortable with yourself and your surroundings as a Jew in West Germany?

That's a question which can best be answered with pathos. For as long as I can remember, I have had a *touche* of the foreigner. I didn't grow up where the majority of others had grown up, and I never had the same mother-tongue as the others. That's why the question 'How does one feel when at home?' occupied me from my earliest years. I have an ugly suspicion that this feeling of being at home is a swindle; maybe it's a conspiracy of the others against me. Another problem is that these manifestations of *Heimatgefühl*[7] always seem almost unpleasant, or even unattractive; I always want to keep myself away from it. When people tell me about the *Glück ihrer Heimat*,[8] my ears automatically close up. I have never experienced anything convincing in this regard. When somebody says to me, 'I like the air in my homeland,' or 'I am one with the region,' or, most convincingly, 'I know there are five people here whose company I would hate to give up,' that much makes sense; but I imagine that those five people could be found in any other place in the world. Another big factor in my moving from the GDR was that most of the people with whom I was involved were aggravated in the same way, so they all moved with me. It was a move *en bloc*, so that basically very little has changed for me; I have almost entirely the same contacts as before. It's only some of the duplicity and some of the animosities which have remained behind; but new ones have sprung up in their place.

History, the past, the Holocaust, survival—survival is different in Der Boxer *than in* Bronsteins Kinder.[9]

What has changed in your way of thinking?

Der Boxer appeared in 1976, and my father died in 1972. You could say that the book has something to do with the death of my father—it's a reaction to it. It's perhaps the desire to create a relationship when it is already too late; everyone has felt the wish to reconstruct something which has only survived in fragments and splinters. I don't think that *Bronsteins Kinder*, which I published ten years later, has any connection with the same motivations.

But it does have to do with the Holocaust and with revenge.

I have often heard discussions and read works dealing with the question of how it was possible that millions of murdered people had for the most part not resisted. One day, an idea for a story came into my mind: about ten or fifteen years ago, three survivors of a concentration camp catch a former guard and take revenge on him. I put this scenario off for a long time as an improbable story or suspense novel, until at a certain point it struck me that actually such a story is quite plausible. Why don't I ever hear about such things? Why don't they ever happen? Why don't I ever learn of them from newspapers or television? Then I asked myself whether the same weariness which at that time hindered a resistance also affects the survivors today. So I wanted to bring to life a story which I consider very probable, but which as far as I know has never happened. Meanwhile, something else came into it: nowadays young people don't want to hear about this sort of topic anymore, about fascism, war and persecution; and I wanted to tell the story from the viewpoint of someone who thinks exactly like that. So the narrator is a young man of this generation who wants to have nothing to do with the old stories; he's not interested in them, and finds them annoying when he's confronted with them. To talk about it in the abstract, I was intrigued by the idea of writing a story about how someone is forced to deal with a subject in which he has no interest, but which still determines his life. I found this perspective exciting.

Let's talk about something different. In this last book you still deal with something which might not be so obvious at first: the son is astonished that he hasn't found out what was going on earlier. The father comes home for dinner and then goes back to torture someone—isn't that in some way a mirror of the past? That is, the Nazi father came home, kissed the children, they all ate dinner, and then he returned to the camp. And how easy it is, not to know what is going on. . . .

I believe that, in human relationships, this is not the exception but the rule. Let me tell you a little story. I know a man who came home one day and found that, after twenty years of marriage, his wife had committed suicide. Fifty years old, she was lying on the floor, and her dentures had fallen out of her mouth and were lying next to her. My acquaintance told me, 'The most devastating thing was that I didn't know she had false teeth.' This is the norm, I think: people hide their most difficult and important problems from one another, and that's what's so terrible.

May I ask you a question to which I already know the answer, but I want it on the record: what do you think of the 'survivor syndrome', the emotional response of those who have survived?

I have encountered what is called the 'survivor syndrome' very seldom, a couple of times in so-called reality, and a few times in so-called art. Perhaps you will be disappointed to hear that I was hardly ever impressed; the way these experiences are presented in almost every medium has very seldom convinced me. Theoretically, I can understand the sense of guilt you feel because, as opposed to others, you've survived; after a while this produces the feeling that you've survived, not as opposed to, but at the expense of others. I myself have good enough reason to feel this: according to reliable information, I survived at my mother's expense. She gave me the little food she had; she starved to death, I didn't. But, just as I said before that I don't know how it feels to be at home, I can also answer that I don't know how it feels to have the survivor syndrome. Perhaps I do have it. In my opinion, the subject has been handled poorly in art; literature about it is most often neither precise enough nor sensitive enough. It's always unrefined—especially as it treats a topic on which neurosurgeons should work, and not butchers who chop off entire arms and legs; but, in most cases, it's the latter which takes place. The German director Eberhard Fechner followed the Majdanek trials in Düsseldorf with his camera for months, or even years, and made a documentary about them. There's a scene in it which impressed me tremendously, during which I came to understand the phenomenon of survivor syndrome better than ever before. A Jewish woman, a witness at the trial, testifies that, as an inmate, she was ordered to take the containers of Cyclone-B gas from a storage room to the *Krematorium*; the Germans then killed the prisoners with this gas. After the woman gives this testimony, the attorney defending an accused female camp-guard enters the plea that the witness should be immediately arrested as an accomplice to murder. There is general outrage over the cynicism and inhumanity of this Nazi-lawyer, when suddenly the woman bursts into tears and says, 'But he is right!' . . . I don't feel comfortable discussing such an event as a film critic would talk about a normal scene in a movie, but when you make your innermost sensitivities public, you have to accept the consequences. And I repeat that, when people tell me about the problems they have with the past, I sit there like a dissatisfied audience.

What do you think of the Historikerstreit?[10]

In the GDR it's considered an incontestable fact that
fascism has economic causes. Although this is just a
part of the answer to how fascism came to be, it's still
an extremely important one, but in the West they keep
on lying about this aspect, or at least they remain
silent about it. Since the end of the war there have
been ceaseless attempts to psychologize fascism, to
emotionalize it, to present the Germans as a kind of
herd which unwittingly found itself under bad shep-
herds. In this connection, fascism is viewed as a mis-
deed standing in a long line of humanity's misdeeds,
or as a reaction to other misdeeds. They talk of the
threat of Bolshevism for Hitler's Germany; that is supposed to be the threat which drove the Nazis to commit their hideous crimes. The most shameless of these
historians say that the threat didn't have to be altogether real; it was enough that Hitler had perceived it
as such. I wouldn't get too upset if such polemics were
conducted by Norwegian or American historians, but
it seems to me that it is Germany which is making all
the attempts to shift responsibility from itself and to
rehabilitate itself retroactively. It isn't an accident
that, during the time of this so-called *Historikerstreit*,
the West German chancellor talked about 'die Gnade
der späten Geburt',[11] which when decoded means,
'From now on we should be allowed to suppress the
past with impunity.' I don't believe that sixty million

Germans simply found themselves under the influence of gangsters. I don't believe that fascism is a mystery, a puzzle which no one can solve. I do believe that in 1933 the Gennan people found themselves in an economic situation which was particularly vulnerable to and ready for the goals and propaganda of Nazism. If one wants to avoid a repetition of it, it must be discussed honestly and mercilessly. As long as the apologists and minimizers and suppressors have their say, as Brecht once said, 'Der Schoss ist fruchtbar noch, aus dem das kroch.'[12]

This is manifested in anti-Semitism.

Not only—they don't need any Jews for that.

Precisely—a real anti-Semite doesn't need any Jews. That's clear. I read the book very carefully . . .

Are you talking about *Der Boxer* or *Bronsteins Kinder?*

No, I'm speaking about the volume Historikerstreit. *There isn't an answer or explanation in it for something which is quite peculiar, namely, the cynicism which was tolerated: the fact that someone made soap out of human fat and that others were made to wash with it, without knowing that the RJF on it stood for 'Reines Jüdisches Fett'.*[13]

The moment you start on a topic like that, these historians will wave a long list of cruelties from the Gulag in your face. For every crime they will have an appropriate countercrime, for every murder a countermurder. Moreover, a very comforting answer is that no one should feel beyond reproach in this matter. People almost everywhere in the world will tell you, when you want to discuss bad conditions in their countries, there's injustice in other countries as well.

There's no spot on earth where, in the course of history, someone hasn't been tortured or killed.

When you accept this as an excuse, there's nothing to discuss with anyone, and all accusations will be meaningless.

Is there such a thing as neo-Nazism without anti-Semitism, since there can be fascism without anti-Semitism? Is there neo-Nazism in your country?

Yes, I believe so. But you shouldn't split this label so easily, because not everyone who believes it's a lie that Jews were murdered in Auschwitz has to be a neo-Nazi—he can just be an idiot. When I was much younger and I wanted to insult someone to the ultimate degree, I called him a fascist. Naturally, this was almost never the real case. When you talk about fascism, you should also have a theoretical view of it.

But neo-Nazism is something entirely different.

Nazism is just one case—the German type of fascism. I think it's necessary to have a combination of situations and preconditions before you can talk about fascism and Nazism. For example, the indiscriminate use of power—this takes place in many places in the world without giving us the right to call it fascism. Another example is racism; however, racism alone is not the same as fascism. Yet another example: in and of itself, the forcible exclusion of any political opposition from a system is still not quite fascism. Again, shall we say aggression against other states? If that alone were to constitute fascism, we should have a great many fascist states in the world. It is peculiar to West Germany that there has never been a determined and powerful reckoning with facism. Reckoning was limited to the declamatory; it was always more in order to placate the worries of the outside world than a real need. So old Nazis, unless they were internationally sought mass-murderers, never had to hide their past. They could be teachers, judges, public prosecutors, politicians, and they have become these in large numbers, and still are, as of today. Of course, they have changed their tune; they don't speak now like they did then. Of course, there's been some pressure exerted on them, but you shouldn't underestimate their influence; their children have grown up under this influence. I consider it even more important that the same industrial works, banks and businesses which financed Hitler and profited by fascism are also in operation today. They too have changed, but more frequently on the outside than in their essence. With all that, I just want to say that the roots of Nazism have not yet died out in West Germany, in

my opinion. I think that, as long as a group does not
find influential financiers for their ideology, this ideology can be unpleasant and threatening, but it will
not conquer the entire society. I have the suspicion
that fascist ideology, even if it is untimely today and
doesn't seem to have a great deal of attraction, has
only been put on ice. You watch it and don't let it
spoil, because you may need it more some other day.
I don't know when, but earlier I considered the threat
of Nazism in West Germany to be nil. Today I believe
that I miscalculated. Perhaps at that time I saw what
I wanted to see. But to return to our starting point, in
West Germany anti-Semitism is officially condemned
and philosemitism has become a state doctrine. While
the unavoidable consequences of this philosemitism
are not so very life-threatening for the Jews, it's still
fire under the same pot, and something always goes
on cooking there.

*Back to literature. Do you have a particular style, or
do you always alter your compositional technique?*

There are writers whom I can identify from a few sentences out of context. There are also writers about
whom I can say that they have their own language,
and that this language is always recognizable in every
one of their books and in every one of the details. I
don't think that you'd recognize the distinctive traits
of my text if you were to read it in fragments. I can
only assume what the reason for this is: whenever I

begin working on a new book—and maybe this is why I begin working on new books less and less frequently—I feel that I have to start from scratch. When I'm writing I never have the feeling that I can build on experience and insight, or on fixed theories. Actually, I always have empty pockets when I sit at my desk. Perhaps this is because I learned the language in which I write at a relatively late age; of course, I don't know this for sure, but I think it's very likely. As a reader, I've always been attracted to the literature of wordplay, which I'm totally incapable of producing. My attempts look ridiculous to me, and I show them to no one. But to mention names, I am delighted with writers like Arno Schmidt or James Joyce, who violate the rules and make a new quality from this violation. In opposition to this, I see myself as someone who always has to prove how well he has learned the rules and how precisely he knows them. I see that you are shaking your head in disagreement—OK. But I am the bird and you are the ornithologist, and of course you have a different view of me than I have of myself.

You say it takes you two to three years to write a book. Do you reduce the text or polish it?

The writing from the first to the last page goes rather fast. When I'm working on a novel, hardly a day goes by when I don't write at least one page, on a good day even two. While I'm writing, I never look at what I've written before in order to change it—only to get information from it.

Like, 'What was that woman's name?'

Exactly. This kind of consistent re-reading is unfortunately very necessary. When I'm working on p. 286, I have to know exactly that there is some detail on p. 34 which will suddenly acquire a meaning; but between these two pages lies a year of work. Therefore, I constantly have to check back in the text, even though, as time goes by, I find this extremely boring. When I'm through with writing the book, that's when all hell breaks loose: I read it from start to finish, I don't like anything and I begin to make changes. Then I read it again from the beginning and make more changes; that's how it goes on and on, until I become afraid that my relationship with the book is becoming destroyed. Suddenly I get this feeling that I could go on with this game of changing for a hundred more years, and something new would always come to my mind; but I no longer have the conviction that it also would mean improvement—it would just be a change. This is the moment when I give the manuscript out of my hand. A reader at the publishing house then looks at it—a person who is very important to me, someone who also makes suggestions. Of course, I am the one who has to make the final decisions, but I need the suggestions. After that I rewrite the book for the last time.

Do you have a blueprint from the very beginning, or does the novel write itself?

I have a concept from the beginning, of course, but during the writing this concept changes. As a matter of fact, with *Bronsteins Kinder* very little was changed. In my study I made a daily schedule on chequered school-paper, so that, unlike all my other books, here the individual days have concrete dates; you can find that a chapter takes place on, say, 3 August 1974. I knew the events for each day precisely; I had to know in what environment my characters moved. Therefore, in *Bronsteins Kinder* only relatively few changes from the original plan were made. In the case of other books, I usually make more. But you shouldn't think that the characters develop their own life while I'm writing, as you often hear it said, and the author just has to write them down; nobody does anything I don't want in my books. However, as I'm progressing in the book, I learn more and more about a character; I can rely on discoveries which I haven't had before. Therefore, I can make wiser decisions than at the beginning; I can also stupidly stick to the first decision, though sometimes I don't.

Where do the unusually finely drawn secondary characters come from? Do they come merely from observation, or from your experiences as script-writer?

I was fascinated by Kafka from a young age, even as a schoolboy. When I ask myself what the most important thing I find in Kafka and nowhere else is, I answer that it's his preoccupation with the sort of details which other authors don't feel are worth their bother. At some point I've realized that these details are the actual topic of literature; at any rate, as an author I want to be preoccupied with the microscopic. Perhaps it's a proof of my own poverty when I tell you that I'd rather be precise than correct; in other words, the conceivable is always more attractive to me than the familiar. Usually, mere observations don't suffice; I actually link several more observations together. I'm afraid I'm a very theoretical type; invented accuracies seem more convincing to me than the ones I actually perceive.

How about the polyphonic stance? Have you ever presented unattractive types as positive characters?

It might surprise you, but my books teem with people I can't stand. I have frequently come across stereotyping in the literature of the GDR which I don't find particularly convincing. It's very boring when an author makes his heroes fight against idiots. Who could get excited or even interested by that? I think it's more important for the success of a book to have precise and convincingly drawn negative characters than heroes.

What do you do with your arcane characters such as the sister in Bronsteins Kinder *or the narrator in* Der Boxer? *They are interesting, they are literary functions which one doesn't recognize as such.*

Here you're right: they are calculations. Of course, I don't mean mathematical calculations—they are narrative calculations. I think that an author has the right to take from his characters exactly what he needs from them. If there's such a thing as economy of prose, then it has to do first of all with reduction. In uninteresting books there are sentences all over which are only there for the sake of completeness. When an author has need of a character's nose, there's no need to tell what colour hair he has. I think that there's nothing which irritates me more in books than this sort of superfluous hair colour. If an author gives a character black hair, he should have a reason for it; the fact that each person has a hair colour isn't good enough. When the hair colour is missing and the reader is interested in it, I'm afraid he has to invent it for himself. After a public reading from *Bronsteins Kinder*, someone asked something about the personality of Hans, and actually wanted to know something that wasn't in the book—whether Hans had some contact with the art of painting. I answered more or less as follows: 'When I tell you a story about a good friend, I don't tell you everything I know about him, only the story itself; that way you can ask me questions, and I can perhaps answer them. But this Hans exists only to the extent that I've invented him, and not one inch further; that is, he exists only in the book, and I don't know any more about him than is in the book. I don't know whether he likes paintings, and if so which ones; and furthermore, it doesn't interest me.'

You write in a reduced, one might even say lapidary manner; I would rather call it the richness of simplicity. The way you deal with adjectives is like the way one deals with weeds—you simply cut them out. I don't know any other German writers who do this, and I find it excellent.

It must be clear that adjectives are, I would say, the landmines of a language; when you step on them, the sentence explodes. Of course, I have to use them responsibly to avoid having nothing by the middle of the book besides dead readers and wounded or offended friends of literature.

Have you ever written poetry?

No, I haven't.

That's what I thought.

But I'm going to tell you about a poem which I did write.

Do you know it by heart?

No, I don't, but I still remember one sentence, which goes, '*Oma und Opa kamen dann in ihren Sonntagskleidern an.*'[14] I have to add something to this. I've often been asked when and how I became a writer. Of course, I have no idea, but it's unpleasant always to answer, 'I don't know.' So I began to make up answers; but whenever I gave them, I didn't like them, and the next time I would make up a new one. Once I gave an answer which didn't sound so stupid, so I repeated it a few times until I began to believe that it was the right one, and this is how it goes. As I said before, I learned German rather late—I was nine when I entered first grade. I probably had a knack for languages, since I learned German relatively quickly. At that time my father was living with a woman; she was a German. I was eleven when the parents of this woman celebrated their silver wedding anniversary. I wrote a poem for this occasion, in which the lines I have just quoted appeared. I showed the poem to my father, and what happened? My father, who naturally loved his only son, treated this poem as if it were by Shakespeare. He not only praised me to the skies for it, but, for the next year or two, he read it aloud to everyone who came to visit the house. There were many people. I stood there, radiant, and was admired by everyone. And so I consciously realized that I was blessed with a gift which only a very few people possess; because of this—so I reasoned—I later became a writer.

Tell me, which of your books did your father live to see?

Only *Jakob der Lügner*,[15] which was unfortunate, since he didn't talk to me for a long time after reading that book. He found it outrageous. His only comment was, 'You can lie to the stupid Germans about the conditions in the Ghetto, but not to me—I was there!'

What is your relationship with German? Is it really true that you now write in a foreign language which has become your native one? Do you have a distance from the language? Do you hear the words differently like Paul Celan did?

I think that, due to learning it later, I have a greater distance from it than a native speaker does; I once wrote that my relationship with the language became even more intensified because of that. Sometimes I talk to people, and they tell me something, and meanwhile I think that they don't have to bother about the language—it just happens. Sometimes I'm envious that they can sit by their linguistic fireside and warm themselves while the text just comes out of them. Unfortunately, this never happens to me; I can never wann myself there. While I'm relating something to you, I have to devote a certain part of my concentration to the production of particular words and sentence structures.

Does this apply to you as a writer, or also as . . .

Also to me as a speaker, not just as a writer. I always have to watch out not to make a mistake out of fear.

That's really astonishing, since you have no accent.

I've had forty-two years for that.

You know, I'm going to die with a heavy accent, although I write much more in English than in Hungarian, and sometimes I find the words more readily.

Did you begin to learn English as a child?

Yes, but with terrible Hungarian pronunciation.

How old were you when you came to America?

Twenty-two.

Well, that's something entirely different. At the age of eight, I was entirely dependent on German—there was no way out.

Well then, it's become your mother-tongue.

It's a pity there's no other word for it—perhaps father-tongue?

Do you tend to write short stories because with this kind of reduction—namely, genuine, total reduction to one experience, one event which changes every-thing—the classical reduction . . .

I was charged once with having an aphoristic rela-tionship with reality. I really do love punchlines, and I know that I'm in danger of sometimes being ready, as they say, to sell my grandmother for the sake of a *bon mot.*

I've written a book of short stories, *Nach der ersten Zufunft*;[16] besides that there are only a few [short stories]. However, you may have noticed that my novels are also full of short stories. Perhaps Germany is a place where short stories aren't very popular, maybe you have to call an *Erzählung*[17] a novel there to be able to sell it. In America it's com-pletely different.

But you are a genuine raconteur.

Yes, I like telling stories. As long as I'm telling stories, someone is listening to me. That's a pleasant feeling.

You were saying that Kafka was your literary model.

No, I wasn't. I have no idea who my literary model was. I can only tell you whom I would read and re-read, and who retains a fascination for me. While I'm working on a novel, there are some works which I have to avoid like the plague, because otherwise my imitative instinct would get loose. Do you know what I read while writing *Bronsteins Kinder*? Goethe's *Dichtung und Wahrheit*,[18] and, in addition to that, his dialogues with von Eckermann. That was great stuff. It interested me fantastically, and was extremely stimulating; and it certainly didn't release any impulse toward imitation. I compared these works with one another, I made a fascinating excursion and it was a spur to my work. I can't read Kafka or Arno Schmidt while I'm writing a book.

To which contemporary writer do you feel an affinity?

I don't feel an affinity to any German writer. When I was still a student and I would read books like normal people do, Max Frisch meant a lot to me.

How about in America or France?

There's an Irish writer, Flan O'Brian, who was a recent discovery for me. Then there's an American writer whom I read not long ago; I was surprised to discover that he's not so well known in America. His name is Walker Percy.

I know nothing about him except his name.

First of all, you should read *The Movie-Goer* and *Love in the Ruins*. . . . Perhaps this is a declaration of capitulation: I'm afraid that lately I can no longer be as impressed by books as I used to be, and this makes me upset. I want that rush in my blood back, but it happens less and less.

Do you read poetry?

Yes, I do.

Perhaps that remains; maybe the magic doesn't disappear so quickly.

I've noticed that I read more collections of letters, biographies and essays, and less and less fiction. I read less and less of the sort of stuff I write myself.

That sounds very pessimistic, but it doesn't come from the fact that you are a writer. . . . I am afraid it comes with age . . . Are you going to write about America?

I don't know. So far I have no plans, and, to tell the truth, I doubt it. It could happen, but I don't feel an obligation to do it. Luckily, experiences don't have to leave the body automatically, like food does. I think I'll keep America to myself, because, no matter how interesting my stay here was, I don't have any reason to write about it.

This interview must not end like this—I must ask one more question. Can one write about the second Bronstein-generation? Is that still a topic?

There are two answers to that. I'm convinced that I'm through with the topic—I don't mean biographically, I mean as someone who has to put sentences, half-sentences and words together about it. I've looked everywhere for them, and I no longer find any. The second answer is that I had the same conviction after I finished *Jakob der Lügner*. Then I thought, 'Never again will you devote yourself to this topic—now you turn toward real life.' I wrote another book about it, and had the same conviction; then I wrote short stories, and I was convinced of the same. Then I wrote yet another novel about it, and I again had the same conviction. Therefore, I believe that this subject is behind me; but this is unreliable information.

Thank you for the conversation.

Notes

1 *Aller Welt Freund* (Everybody's Friend), 1982.

2 *Irreführung der Behörden* (Misleading the Authorities), 1975.

3 A position similar to assistant manager.

4 A technical term referring to someone employed in commerce.

5 In *Aller Welt Freund*

6 *Der Boxer* (The Boxer), 1976.

7 Feeling (snugly) at home.

8 The bliss of their homeland.

9 *Bronsteins Kinder* (Bronstein's Children), 1986 (English translation, 1987).

10 Current debate among West German historians regarding the idiosyncratic nature of the Holocaust.

11 'The grace of being born too late.'

12 'The womb from which it crept out is still fertile.' Bertolt Brecht, *Kriegsfibel* in *Gesammelte Werke in acht Bänden*, VOL. 4 (Frankfurt am Main, 1967), p. 1048.

13 'Pure Jewish Fat.'

14 'Then came Grandpa and Grandma dressed in their Sunday best.'

15 *Jakob der Lügner* (Jakob the Liar), 1976.

16 *Nach der ersten Zukunft* (After the First Future), 1980.

17 Novelette, long short story.

18 *Aus meinem Leben*; *Dichtung und Wahrheit* (From My Life; Poetry and Truth).

It is a dreadful defeat for socialism that, 72 years after the October Revolution, McDonald's is about to set up in Moscow and celebrate its triumph. This is meant as anything but a joke. A long chain of misguided developments has brought the majority of people in socialist countries to assume the Western world to be a source of conveniences and socialism the place where inconveniences are growing. Today socialism is beginning to feel just how right Marx was when he wrote that being determines consciousness, not the other way around. For decades people neglected this truth, but now resources, which were used to subsidize this life-long illusion, are running low. This is good.

Doubts are emerging as to whether a theory can be realized, that appears wonderfully reasonable in its premises and conclusions, but assumes that humans are reasonable beings, capable of being guided by their findings. The opposing social system, which does not require any theory, but rests on the assumption that humans are malicious, ruthless and violent, is celebrating triumphs, particularly since supposedly socialist states have never tried to prove that there is a different way. All of a sudden, this becomes clear.

The end of the socialist idea would be the end of confidence, not necessarily of individual confidence, which appears to be founded on the hope that the statistical feasibility of misfortune will strike one's neighbour rather than oneself. Rather it would be the end of societal confidence.

There will be many who think that we have spent enough time striving after some rather eccentric ideals, that daydreams cannot last forever and that we need to get down to business, everyone to his own. They will be quick to join the ranks of those they recently thought to be political hardheads, those who filled them with disgust.

However, those who want to continue have no choice but to see the real existing socialism as a miscarriage, at most as an attempt, which is of no other use than to demonstrate its failure. The socialist theory of the future must not content itself with making ends meet and excusing the shortcomings of the present as a result of the past. Above all, it will have to concern itself with one question that did not seem to exist until now: How will humanity be able to work its way out of the situation it's gotten itself into without dying out in the process?

If the answer is that there is no way, then there is no need for a socialist theory. This means the social-ists are confronted with a task which most people see as impossible to solve. This is not a dramatically new situation for them.

If socialism is eliminated from the spectrum of possible ways of life, we reach the point where, in my opinion, the spirit of doom really begins.

Translated by Jonathan Becker

'Really existing socialism' is on the way out, no question. Good thing too, if you fix your mind on the true condition of life in the socialist states, and not the fictional version which their leaders have passed off as the truth. The West has won—and there's the rub.

Here in the West, we live in societies that have no particular goal or objective. If there is any guiding principle, it's consumerism. In theory, we can increase our consumption until the planet lies about us in ruins and, given current trends, that's precisely what will happen. In spite of everything we knew and understood about them, we had a hope that the socialist states might find a different path. That hope is gone. People there are desperate to adopt the principles of the West: the conversion of as many goods as possible into rubbish (which is what consumption means), and the free expression of all types of ideas (accompanied by a growing reluctance to think at all). Converts are

liable to be especially strict and zealous in the obser-
vance of their new faith; I expect the same will apply
to the people of these recently converted nations.

A few days ago, I was talking to a friend about
the possibility of German reunification, the conversation that all Germans have been having these past
days and weeks. He was in favour of it, I was against.
After a while he lost his temper with me, and asked
me how I could possibly justify the continued existence of the German Democratic Republic. I started
thinking, and I'm still thinking now. If I can't think of
any reasons, I shall have to change my mind and
become a supporter of reunification. I shall have to be
in favour of turning Eastern Europe into an extension
of Western Europe.

The only argument I am able to come up with is
perhaps more suitable for a poem than a political discussion: the most important thing about socialist
states isn't any tangible achievements, but the fact
that they give us a chance. Things are not cut and
dried as they are here. The uncertainty there doesn't
promise anything, of course, but it's our only hope for
the continued existence of humanity. Eastern Europe
looks to me like one last attempt. And when it's over,
it'll be time to withdraw our money from the bank,
and start hitting the bottle in earnest.

Translated by Michael Hofmann

When I was two years old I came to this ghetto. At age five, I left it again, headed for the camp. I don't remember a thing. This is what people told me, this is what is in my papers, and this was, therefore, my childhood. Sometimes I think: What a shame that something else is not written there. At any rate, I know the ghetto only from meagre hearsay.

My father talked to me about it a few times, reluctantly and seldom. During his lifetime I was not curious enough to outsmart him with subtle questions and then it was too late. Nevertheless, I wrote stories about the ghettos as if I were an expert. Perhaps I thought that, if I could only write long enough, the memories would come. Perhaps at some point, I even began to take some of my inventions for memories. Without memories of childhood, it is as if you are condemned to constantly carry around with you a box whose content you do not know. And the older you get, the heavier the box feels and the more impatient you become to finally open it.

Now the floor of my room is littered with the photos of this exhibition. If I had memories, they would have to be at home there, on those streets, behind those walls, among these people. The women in the pictures interest me most: I don't know what my mother looked like. No photos of her exist. She died in the camp. I could just choose one of the women, I suppose. My father said that she was strikingly pretty, of course.

Most of the pictures convey a tranquility for which we yearn. They radiate peacefulness. In my eyes, they depict something of *the good old days*. The photographer seems to have been striving to prove that the ghetto was not as gruesome a place as enemy propaganda might have insinuated, that things happened there as they do among the rest of humanity. Even though these people were a bit peculiar, a bit different. But we knew that before. If we look closely, we might even think that the ghetto was a place of meditation.

The young Jewish policeman, who examines the paperwork of a suspicious looking passer-by, as is the duty of police officers all over the world. The barber, who has taken off his cap in front of the photographer and waits for customers in front of his wooden house, which is certainly comfortable on the inside.

The bearded man, who pulls a wagon with rubber tires over the cobblestones. The worker, who isn't exactly killing himself. Even the four Jews, who carry a dead person alongside a wall, don't deserve more than a brief moment of pity. Carrying a corpse with four people can't be all that hard and death happens everywhere. We might actually have more sympathy for the German guard next to the sentry box, standing there so far from home and so lost. It is so damn lonely at the entrance to the ghetto. No one wants to go in and no one out. The pictures suggest that everything is carefully regulated here, in a manner deeply inherent to the things and people.

With one word, I think up theories of the objectives of the photographer. I see through his intentions; the guy can't fool me. But all of a sudden, something happens that unsettles me. Individual pictures absorb my gaze. I fall into them, far from having the intention to write a text. I see two pictures of children. In the first, they wait for rations to be handed out, pots and little buckets and spoons in hand. In the second, they are wearing red caps and staring at the photographer. Interrupted at play and nonetheless motionless. No, a child as small as I must have been then is not to be seen. But there are probably children in the pictures like the ones who knew me, who took things away from me, or beat me up or ordered me around. Perhaps there is someone standing there who would be my best friend today, had things taken a slightly more favourable course.

I hate sentimentalities. They cloud the mind. I would prefer to close up all of the holes from which they might crawl. Each time my father was overcome by emotion, I left the room until he got a hold of himself again. Suddenly that does not play a role anymore. The pictures fill me with emotion, me of all people, and I have to wipe the most ridiculous tears from my eyes. No girls in the photos, just boys, boys and more boys. Why is that? Is that the reason that girls have, as far back as I can remember, always been special creatures to me?

In one of the pictures, Jewish firefighters drive through the ghetto. What was it about those firefighters? My father told me something, that they existed, that he knew one of them, or that they always came too late, or that there was always something burning. I have forgotten even that. Constantly I have the feeling that I simply need to make a bit more of an effort to remember, instead of waiting lazily and lethargically for the memories to come to me. But I make an effort until I go crazy, and nothing comes. Only the pictures lie in my room, so incomprehensibly near.

When I received them, when I opened the package and began to spread them out, I soon had the sense that I needed to put them in a different order. But, in what kind of an order? What belonged to what and what should be separated? Do children belong with children and bearded men with bearded men and tradesmen with tradesmen? And police officers with police officers and blondes with blondes? In any case, the order isn't right. It's like a crack in a plate that ruins the most beautiful shot. I order and re-order the pictures over and over again. I want to solve the puzzle. I put the train station on the outside, the cemetery on the outside, the streets in the centre, wooden houses together, stone houses together, the workshops in between, the border on the border. Again and again everything is wrong. The little lamp of memory doesn't illuminate.

I stare at the pictures and search for that one decisive piece of my life until my eyes are sore, but only the vanishing lives of the others are recognizable. To what ends should I speak of outrage or sympathy? I want to descend to them and do not find the way.

Translated by Martin Bäumel and Tracy Graves

A few weeks ago, I watched an interview on television with a famous singer from East Germany. The conversation was filled with conviviality and reunification-bliss. The mood darkened at only one point when an ugly memory came up. It was mentioned that the singer had taken part in a commemorative event held by the GDR government at the 'Palace of the Republic' a couple of months earlier, on 7 October 1989, in celebration of the fortieth anniversary of the state's formation. The singer appeared quite remorseful as he explained how he came to participate in such an event. The party had enlisted the crème de la crème of the country's artists to perform on that night and it was basically a case of superior orders. The singer named a few celebrities who had also been a part of this disgrace. It seemed that he was in good company. Anyway, it became clear that he had not taken the stage out of his own free will, but only because he *had to*.

His explanation satisfied the interviewer, who asked no further questions about how the singer was coerced into attending. If one *has to*, there is nothing to be done. These are superior orders. By now, everyone should be well aware of the depravity the party was capable of, so there is no need to go into detail. This *I had to* has become unbeatable. Whoever says it is safe from further possibly embarrassing questions. Aren't there enough examples of the party's dealings with its opponents? There was only one efficient defense: not being an opponent.

Just so there is no misunderstanding: It is none of my business where that singer performed and where he didn't, what he took part in and what he didn't. Courage is not an enforceable quality. But it becomes a different matter if he stands up and says he had no choice other than being a conformist.

It is a known fact that disobeying directives is uncomfortable. It is a known fact that it consumes energy and brings trouble when one attempts to counter the will of a powerful state with one's own. It would be great if insurgency was honoured and conformity punished, wouldn't it? The world would be full of dissidents self-consciously giving their governments or their bosses a piece of their mind. But unfortunately the only way for non-conformity to be effective is if there are enough non-conformists to actually change the way things are.

Without a doubt the people of the GDR were subjected to an exceptionally strong oppressive force. If there was no other evidence for this, one would only need to mention the regular election result of ninety-nine per cent, which is not only beyond the realm of plausibility, but also incredibly shameless. Even members of the politburo had to cut back on their personal ambitions in such a way that it turned their stomachs. When asked why he lived in Wandlitz,[1] for example, Kurt Hager, the attorney general of GDR culture, replied: How could anyone seriously believe that he had done so of his own accord? How could anyone not see that this was a case of forced internment, the third such forced internment during his lifetime, by the way? How could anyone not imagine that he would have favoured living in the country, with the people, where life is? Suddenly it became clear that even the members of the politburo were victims of the politburo.

Seriously, an alarm system had been installed, which marked everyone who conducted himself in a non-authorized way and, on top of that, there was a system of punishments, light, medium and exceedingly harsh. The way that the state dealt with its populace was nothing out of the ordinary for Germany. At the time, the Stalinist occupying power only had to keep going where the Nazis had left off, and the party, as soon as the GDR was founded, continued that business seamlessly. I would dare claim that the obligation to conform was perceived as being a lot stronger by the citizens of the GDR than it was in the Third Reich, especially because it is likely that people identified much more with the Nazi state than, later on, with the GDR. I cannot imagine that the NSDAP [Nationalsozialistische Deutsche Arbeiterpartei— National Socialist German Workers' Party; aka Nazi Party] would have been rejected by voters in free elections to the same extent that the SED [Sozialistische Einheitspartei Deutschlands—Socialist Unity Party of Germany] was recently, not even shortly after the war.

Some dictatorial regimes hit it lucky with their population while some draw a blank. The measure of repression they have to employ depends fully on the unruliness of the citizenry. Its not like oppressors oppress for the fun of oppressing. They like nothing better than a people that is so intimidated or corrupted that it unquestioningly follows every instruction. It makes life look harmonious, it allows them to claim that the sun of unity is shining over the country. And, whenever individual troublemakers kick up a fuss anyway, they can be brought to reason without causing a great stir. If need be, such regimes can even be generous and leave it at the wag of a finger. But only if the instances of troublemaking are isolated enough.

In this respect the GDR government was quite lucky. They had to deal with a population that was exceedingly willing to be subservient, with citizens whose main act of resistance was being annoyed. When we compare the massive degree of rejection and the level of hatred toward the party that articulated itself after the reunification with the insurgency it had to face during the forty years before, we observe a certain lack of symmetry. I do not believe that the revelations of the last few months have produced any new fundamental insights about the inner workings of the GDR. Even though some of the discovered details might be breathtaking, they do not add anything that was not basically known already. It was known that the country's natural resources were ransacked in the most irresponsible ways. It was known that the only part of the economy that functioned efficiently was widespread cronyism. It was known that surveillance, coercion and bullying at any cost were everywhere. And it was known that the party leadership was not made up of the most selfless or the most intelligent people. Anyone could see, and saw, that the emperor wasn't wearing any clothes. But, since shouting 'Look, the emperor is naked!' is no longer a punishable offense, it is now being celebrated as the most valuable of insights.

One of the most passionately discussed topics in the GDR is the question of how former employees of the state security service should be dealt with. The scale of views ranges from *lock them up* to *forget about them*. I admit that I would be completely stumped were I held responsible for deciding the fate of these dreadful and sometimes pitiful people. All the opinions that I have heard so far have been my own at least for a few seconds at one time or another. But what a lousy situation it is to be shaken by one's own emotions and unable to find a foothold in a solid opinion. Lock them up or forget about them or what?

The wrath with which the Stasi is confronted everywhere in the dying GDR was sparked by the agency itself, of course. Everyone was at its mercy and even those who were left alone had to think anxiously: For how much longer? Everything was recorded, sighs, short tempers, sullen looks. Often the gentlemen appeared openly, without the disguise usual in these services, as if the consciousness of their omnipresence was more valuable to them than the information they gathered. In every government office there were people working for the Stasi, in every club, in every school, in every nursery, in many families. People accepted them as an irritating part of their environment, like smog. One of their greatest successes consisted in the fact that people assumed they were present in places they were not. Many phone calls were made mainly with regard to those intercepting them. Letters contained phrases that were not addressed to the recipient, but to the inspector. And, at assemblies (everyone's life was full of assemblies), people applauded and were sickened by the fact that they did. Reasons for the rage, which is now being unloaded on the cursed Stasi, are easy to find.

And still, I feel that this rage has an awkward aftertaste, that it is not always honest. It appears to me that the zeal with which many people decry and prosecute the harassments of the Stasi is an attempt to undo their own servility. The more terrifying the menace looming over everyone is depicted, the more likely one's own conformity is to be deemed appropriate. If you played the perfect subordinate for them, shouldn't you at least be allowed to think you had no choice?

All the same, this is an important question—was there no other choice? I doubt this and I believe it would not have demanded superhuman qualities to resist. I do not know where this would have led. Maybe it would have simply led to more repression. Maybe it would have intensified conflicts (which were quite rare in the GDR) and, as a result, could have brought some change to the stagnant conditions. Maybe it could even have led to a society with more freedoms. That seems to be the most probable assumption to me. In any case, the forty years of the GDR would have been a time of less frustration, hypocrisy and injustice.

During the mid-1960s I met an old classmate who, I had heard, was working for state security. We had a few drinks. I was afraid to decline his invitation and I was also curious. As he got a bit drunk, I asked him straight out if the stories about him were true and he smilingly confirmed. He was absolutely not coerced into it, he went on to say, answering a second question which I hadn't even asked yet. The pay was good, the work was bearable, sometimes even interesting, and he had been assigned a good apartment which he would have had to wait years for otherwise. The more we drank, the more outspoken he became. I don't remember everything; I had to keep up the drinking as well. Anyway, he soon acted like I was reproaching him for being a snitch (which I would never have dared) and defended himself. Meaning he attacked me. Like so many other sentimental dumbasses I was suffering from delusions just because the state security service had observed some people. The thing we were unable to comprehend was that people *had to* be watched. If only he felt the slightest sympathy for those people, he would look for a different job in an instant, he told me. But, no matter how long he thought about it, he found no reason to like them. He listed a number of characteristics, all common and frequently described in world literature, for which, in his opinion, people deserved to be despised. At one point he said: 'They could take us out with the snap of a finger. They would only need to shake themselves

intensely once and they would be rid of us. But for
that they are too gutless. We control and they *let*
themselves be controlled. It takes two to spy.'

It is a fact that the Stasi was able to operate largely without interference. As we now know, the most
significant handicap it had to deal with was the intel-
ligence quotient of its boss. No one got in its way,
hardly anyone objected to its impertinences and it was
left to its own devices as if it was the long arm of fate.
If there is no disagreement for a long period of time, it
comes to the point where that lack of disagreement
can be interpreted as approval. It was easy to draw
this mistaken conclusion in the GDR and a section of
the party leadership, probably the majority, drew it.

If the submissiveness with which most citizens of
the GDR endured their government is retrospectively
declared as *inevitable* submissiveness or even silent
opposition, the new era begins with lies. No, bravery
and honesty were not ranked highly in those forty
years. This is not meant as an accusation against the
people, no one is obliged to be brave, but it should not
be concealed either. The pressure everyone was
exposed to did not necessarily have to lead to total submission. And this submission should not be justified
solely on the grounds that insubordination would have
led to discomfort. Having to live with the memory of
one's own timidity is the price one pays for decades of
yeasaying. And many are not prepared to pay it.

When it comes to explaining undesirable societal developments, the Germans have a special obligation to be precise. Actually no, nonsense, every nation has this obligation; the Germans just have it too. Attempts are still being made to cart the guilt for Nazi Germany's crimes to the Führer Headquarters and unload it there. It is a wonderful kind of absolution to hold Hitler fully responsible for everything the Germans did during the war and the six years preceding it, for every denunciation, every injustice, every shot in the neck.

Now I do not want to roll out this comparison and draw undue parallels between the Third Reich and the GDR. But I do wish to denounce this method of absolution. That is just what the opportunists wish for, that their compliance is forgotten overnight and they find themselves standing there as victims who had this insurmountable force breathing down their necks. Well, the force was there, and it was breathing down their necks and it was strong as well, but insurmountable? We were just getting to the point where we stopped believing that people are simply products of their environment, nothing but dust blown around by fate. Real existing Ssocialism was a common effort realized by the party leadership, its henchmen and all those who obeyed. The fact that it prospered to the liking of some and much to the dislike of others doesn't change the fact that all those involved had a part in shaping it.

The phrase 'coming to terms with the past' has been around for a long time. It is a linguistic drape that approximates a thought without disclosing it. I, for one, never understood what is concealed behind this phrase, but I had an intense premonition: the desire to deal with the past in a way that stops it from tormenting us. This desire appears understandable to me and it is legitimate as well. In my opinion though, there is only one way to get there. We must keep the past in our memory and not lie about it to ourselves. The more that time passes without remembering, the harder the task becomes. And, if we are not watchful, one day everyone will have their own version of the past and will have acted in a way that is favourable and honest.

Yet another GDR story: One day a fellow author showed me a manuscript for a novel and asked me for my opinion. It must have been sometime in the late 1970s. After reading the text, I asked whether he had offered it to any East German publishers yet. He shook his head. I told him to save his breath, no GDR publisher would ever dare to bring it before the censor. I told him that, if he was seriously considering publishing it, he should go straight to a West German publisher. That was what he had in mind, he told me sadly. He was just waiting for the right time. What time, I asked him. He replied that his daughter was just about to take her final exams in school and that I should be able to imagine how she would fare if the book was published in West Germany now. How could I not understand?

A few months later after his daughter had passed her exams, I inquired again about the novel. He said he would have to wait a while before publishing it unfortunately. He was in the process of buying a house and the proceedings for approval were under way. He was very reliant on the benevolence of the authorities. The next time I asked him, his daughter was waiting to be admitted to the university. The time after that he and his wife had applied for permission to take a trip to Egypt. This trend continued on for a pretty long time. A couple of months ago, it appeared to him that the time was finally right. He offered the novel to a publisher, but no one was interested in it anymore.

Translated by Jonathan Becker

Note

1 Wandlitz is a small town outside of Berlin where high-ranking GDR officials lived removed from society in highly secure and relatively luxurious homes.

When I was writing my first book *Jacob the Liar* over twenty years ago, I did not wonder for a second why I was writing it. I thought the story was good enough for a first novel. It seemed to fit into the German context and I could hear the tone in which I wanted to tell it. People were going to like it, at least those people who knew something about the trade. And, if they felt challenged or provoked because someone was telling a story about things as terrible as life in the ghetto and the persecution of the Jews, not in the usual tearful voice, but using humour, then all the better. At the time, I believed that being provocative was probably the best approach a writer could take, all the more so because I lived in an environment where most writers were doing the opposite. Furthermore, I was already thirty years old and it was about time for me to start on a novel if I did not want my plans for the future to fizzle out. I do not believe that I began

writing the book because of my relationship to literature, but rather because I wanted to be a writer.

I was convinced that I was about to begin useful
work and did not deem it necessary to analyse this
optimistic assumption. I considered myself capable of
insights. I was determined to write only meaningful
words and to pen no sentence that was not necessary
or beautiful. Therefore, I had no doubt that readers,
possibly readers all over the world, would benefit
from my novel in many different ways. Imagine this:
There is a relatively young man who has not attracted
anybody's attention with his literary production—if
only because he has never produced any literature—
and this man sits down at a table to write books and
does so with the conviction that it would be a loss for
humanity if he did not.

We can quickly determine whether this young
man's conviction was justified. Of course it wasn't. Of
course he was a megalomaniac and of course the
impact of the finished book, in comparison with his
high expectations, was close to zero. This aside, it is
more important that we figure out the reasons for
his inordinate fearlessness—whether or not there
was something more to it than the excessive self-
confidence occasionally found among young men. I
think I can remember that there was something, even
if I am barely able to describe that something in
detail.

Before we start, I should probably say that I consider such self-overestimation bordering on arrogance an indispensable tool of writers. But don't think this means that I believe writers should find every foolish thought that crosses their minds valuable or treat every idea like a treasure. We all know that our first thoughts on a subject have the unfortunate tendency to be moronic, so that's definitely not what I'm talking about. What I'm getting at here is that writers must value their creations and know that a lot depends on the result of their efforts. There is, I suspect, no other way to produce literature worthy of being called literature. I am convinced that no significant book has ever been written by an author who thought his work didn't really matter all that much or that it wouldn't make a big difference whether or not he wrote his novel, play or poem.

Of course, a writer's technical talent, that is, his relationship to language and his ability to turn his musings into words, is not necessarily linked to his confidence. But, if a writer does not feel some sense of self-importance, a back door opens without him even realizing it. And, through this back door, arbitrariness and opportunism and artificiality, in any case triviality, sneak their way into his books. The certainty that, when his troubles are over, an insight or a sentiment or an intuition that did not exist before might appear is a constant incentive for the author. It keeps him going during his long and solitary work. In fact, it keeps him going much more than any prospect of royalties ever could. Remember that the decision to lock oneself up in a room for two years and to try and get an initially vague thought down on paper really and truly requires courage. And the most favourable circumstances are necessary so that the endeavour is not abandoned along the way. The most important of these circumstances, I cannot emphasize it enough, is the knowledge of the great significance of the text that is about to be written.

I am aware that I am talking about a mindset that could also be called a behavioural disorder or even a mental defect. Even so, I declare this mindset to be the precondition of authorship. I am also aware that many people think otherwise, that they think the business of writing can have all possible preconditions except for that one. But I think they are wrong and they fail to see the obvious.

The young man I once was, whom I try to remember now, was perhaps lacking many other preconditions, but definitely not overconfidence. It is not that he chose to be overconfident because he thought it would bring him more success. He had not thought at all about the fact that his delusions of grandeur might be beneficial to his plans; he simply had those delusions. Back then, when someone asked him how in the world he could dare consider himself a novelist or when a well-meaning friend pointed out that he should spend his time on a more promising project, he just smiled and said nothing. At those moments, he felt like the frog that already knows about the kiss that will turn him into a prince. He was full of confidence.

Confidence meant two things. On the one hand, it was the certainty that one was capable of mastering the intended task. On the other hand, and much more importantly, it was the conviction that the future warranted investing all this effort. The belief that the future would, without any doubt, be superior to the present, that there was an unstoppable, irreversible change for the better, that possible setbacks along the way were annoying but couldn't change the fact that our society, that humanity, was moving in the right direction. *That* is confidence. In the end, it constitutes a kind of basic trust that human beings are capable of acting in accordance with their insights, that they value the growth of civilization above any other form of growth. If we know that human progress is endangered and we understand the danger and the ways of dealing with it, it would be insane to think we are facing our doom. That's how I felt at the time. And I wasn't the only one who felt that way either. It was the basic conviction of those times. Not only has this trust vanished, I am now willing to bet anything that it is the other way around.

What has driven us all completely insane is the realization that the consequences of our actions affect us only partially but impact our children so much more. Nowadays, it seems that more and more people think we don't need to worry about future generations because there won't be that many of them anyway. And the more we continue on in this way, the better the chance this assumption has of becoming reality. Physiologically, the inability of the body or its individual parts to carry out the brain's orders is called *movement disorder* or, in severe cases, *paralysis*. It seems to me that our societies, without any exception, are paralysed. Insights don't count for anything and our ability to use them to guide us atrophies. That doesn't mean we don't constantly seek out and collect new insights. On the contrary, we amass real mountains of knowledge. More and more, this activity has come to resemble a game that is of no importance outside the salon. Psychologically, such behaviour is called schizophrenia. The knowledge-industry is suffering from over-production; it must reduce its capacity. So there is a mountain of insights lying around, we feel bad about it and we have no idea what to do.

I don't want to misuse this occasion to spread doom and gloom, especially not when you have been kind enough to award me a prize and I should speak light-heartedly. I simply arrived at this horrible topic because I am talking about myself. I am worried, you see. I mean—what's happening with me worries me. The fear that our time on earth is slowly coming to an end is taking a toll on my writing. Perhaps this feeling is just another of those many delusions of grandeur I described earlier. If that's the case, they won't help me this time. It is becoming increasingly difficult for me to convince myself that it would be a horrible loss if I didn't sit down and write a new book and try to get to the bottom of this or that story. What's even more disturbing, I am hardly able to consider whatever I do of the least importance anymore.

You could say, of course, that I have finally come to my senses and recognized, however late, my limits. There might be some truth in that, but it would be a minor reason at most. I am self-assured enough to claim that my achievements as a writer, however disappointing they might be, are not remotely as depressing as the achievements of humankind. Literature can recover from the former. From the latter, the world cannot. My supply of confidence, my only tailwind, is used up. It never really attracted my attention while I had it anyway. One day, as I saw myself in the window, sitting at my desk and working on a book, I began to feel strange. I imagined that I was someone who was safely watering his little herb garden while an earthquake was raging all around him.

I would never claim that there are only altruistic motives for writing or that the writer works in the service industry and should mainly attend to the dissemination of insights. He is full of personal, private, intimate reasons and without these reasons he'd be lost from the start. But suddenly, it seems to me, there are *only* such reasons because none of the others seem to make sense any more. The writer who is still trying to be an active part of social processes appears anachronistic and pitiful; his texts reek of a lack of sophistication. He is apparently unable to understand that his sense of commitment is neither promising nor of any importance to anyone. He can only survive as an isolated being, at best marginally concerned about the big picture, a part-timer, so to speak. There is no escaping the every-man-for-himself society. In this situation, a writer might have strange ideas. For instance, he might think it is a good idea to begin writing screenplays for a TV series.

I didn't have to overcome any of my scruples to do that. On the contrary, it felt like a little piece of salvation. After all, I was looking for a job that didn't require any confidence and, the moment I was given the opportunity, I knew this was it. I was convinced that I could do the job well. I thought it would suit me to write dialogues and to be a little funny and to make the characters appear fairly true-to-life, even more so because competition in this field was not something of which I was afraid. So I wrote 'Liebling Kreuzberg'.[1] I spent two and a half years on it. I wrote one episode after the other, simply because I could.

When I was in college, there was a young man in my class who was widely considered to be an over-achiever. He certainly was one too. Once, during a seminar, Professor Georg Klaus asked the students a question and this young man raised his hand to respond, was given the floor and gave his answer. Professor Klaus thought about it for a moment and then said: 'You only said that because it's right.' It was one of the most devastating verdicts I have ever heard. I remembered this story when I had to decide how many more screenplays I wanted to write for 'Liebling Kreuzberg'.

I quit when business was thriving. A few of my friends couldn't believe it at first and the producer was speechless: What the hell had gotten into me, giving up on a business that was running so smoothly? People probably thought, 'Finally he found something he can actually do without too much trouble and immediately he is too good for it!' That wouldn't have been too far from the truth. But one of my annoying personality traits got in the way, perhaps my last remaining writer's habit: the behavioural disorder I talked about earlier. It prevailed over my interest in money or material things and gave me a desire for more demanding work. You probably understand that it is much more satisfying to roam around in exciting foreign territory than to go for the same walk around the block over and over again. Writing only becomes an adventure when one nears the limits— one's own, preferably. Even if I never advance that far, I knew for sure at that moment that my limits lay far outside a lawyer's office in Kreuzberg.

So I will sit down again and write a novel and cancel out everything I said before. At the most, I have provided evidence that I am also not capable of following my own insights. But, I must say, who would have expected anything else? Once, I had a torn muscle in my leg, and I remember tossing and turning in bed for nights on end, hoping a new position might help ease the pain. I should have known that this was useless. I should have known that I could toss and turn any way I wanted, it wouldn't make the pain in my leg go away. But, while I was rolling from one side to the other again and again, I was convinced that my salvation lay in finding the right position.

I thank you all very much for this award. It is like a tailwind for me. It encourages me to think about this whole confidence thing once again.

Translated by Martin Bäumel and Tracy Graves

Note

1   'Liebling Kreuzberg' was a television show that
    ran for three seasons from 1986 until 1989 and
    again for two seasons in 1993 and 1997. The
    dramatic comedy follows the work and life of the
    anti-hero Robert Liebling, a lawyer in the
    Kreuzberg district of Berlin.

That I stand before you as someone who is considered to be a German author is the result of a series of coincidences. I was born in Poland in the drab city of Łódź, the child of parents, as they say, of Jewish background. That is, whether I want it or not, also my background. And if soon after my birth the German army had not come, if it had not occupied the country and later put my parents and me in a ghetto and later in various concentration camps, if the Red Army had not freed the Sachsenhausen camp, where I sojourned at the end, then I'd like to know as what and before whom I would be standing today. But that's not the least of remarkable facts.

After the war my father, next to me the other survivor of my family, remained curiously in Berlin. Could he not have emigrated to Brooklyn, where perhaps I would have become an American writer? Or to Buenos Aires or, which is not entirely beyond the realm of the imagination, to Tel Aviv? But no, he

decided for what I consider the most exotic of all possibilities, he remained here, moved into an apartment
only a few subway stops from the entrance to the
camp and arranged for me to become a German. He
didn't even want to go back the few miserable kilome-
tres to Poland, where he had met a few friends or
acquaintances, even if he had no more relatives.

Believe me, later, when I understood the whole
significance of the matter, I made my father's life difficult with questions. I thought I had the right to find
out why we had landed on Lippehner Straße 5 in East
Berlin and not somewhere else in the world. But he
remained silent, cast up his eyes, and left me standing
as though he could deflect my question only in that
way, a question that probably sounded in his ears like
a reproach. But in doing that I had no intention of
remonstrating him; I wanted only to shed light on a
matter that was not exactly without significance for
my life.

Once, only a single time, did he deign to give me
a kind of answer, even if a pretty thin one; it was in
the mid 1950s. He lay in bed for months with a stomach ulcer, and I sat for hours every day in his room,
ready to hand him things or go on errands or talk. In
a situation like that it is not unusual, out of a lack of
variety or simply lack of ideas, that you start to talk
about things that were considered previously as
checked off. I told my father that he still owed me an

answer, and he said: 'Are you starting that again?' And I said that I was continually asked in school and in the sport club and by all kinds of people why we had not returned to Poland (that was an outright lie; even until today not a single person except for my son has asked about that). Anyway, I asserted that and added that I had to remain silent at such questions or think up one lie or another, and he said that there was nothing worse for ulcers than excitement. But I wouldn't be shrugged off so easily, not this time; it seemed my last chance. I said that he could get rid of me playfully, but he had to do one thing for me: Finally tell me why he did not want to live in Poland anymore after the war.

He looked at me unhappily, like you look a tormenting spirit from whom there is no escape. Then he said softly: 'Can't you *really* answer that yourself?' I shook my head. And he sighed at such a lack of understanding and said: 'Did the Polish anti-Semites lose the war or the Germans?' Then he turned over on his back and closed his eyes, as though the reply had exhausted him extremely.

So I have to thank my father's belief that here, in this part of the world, he was somewhat safe from persecutions for my becoming a German. By the way, this belief also kept him from going to West Germany; he often got upset about how well Nazis got along there; the names Oberländer and Globke were familiar to me when I was a child. Only one thing interested him in the Soviet zone of occupation and later in the GDR: that the anti-fascists were in control there. And when someone dared to criticize the behaviour of *his* Russians or the conditions in their part of Germany, he considered him either a malcontent or an enemy. Differentiations were not his strength; indeed, he considered the fussy observation of societal details to be a trick with which his opponents wished to create advantages. He felt encircled by enemies.

We did not count as immigrants from the beginning, rather as a kind of homecomer; for my father had been born in Bavaria, and as a small boy had moved East with his parents. That simplified the procedure of remaining here enormously. Still, our move here had naturally nothing to do with coming home; from the first second I felt like an outsider, not only because I had to learn the language first. Not only because we were issued a better foodstuffs card than the others. Not only because we had the pleasure of a friendliness that even I recognized as hypocritical. My father placed value on the status of the foreigner; somehow or other he wanted to belong to the occupational power; he paid careful attention to never erasing the differences between us and the others. He spoke continually of *the Germans* as the others, and hardly a day passed on which he did not utter judgements about them: The Germans always had two opinions—one for the front and one for the rear. Whether the Germans were pleasant or horrible depended on what kind of orders they received. The Germans learned fast and forgot even faster. The Germans loved the strong and despised the weak. He asked: 'How do the Germans treat you at school?' He taught me to live like an onlooker, and when one day he believed he recognized that I no longer liked that attitude, he said: 'Just let them feel that you don't belong to them—they'll not ever forget it anyway.'

Of course, my father tried everything to make his distributions of likes mine also; he wanted me to see dangers where he saw them, for me to expect my well-being from those from whom he expected them himself, and naturally he was not without success in these efforts. Presumably his influence on me has even today not died out, so that I will never know when I sound like him and when like myself.

Recently I read in the newspaper that a judge from Bautzen had to answer to a federal court, a jurist from the early time of the GDR who tossed off frightful decisions that had punished not according to law but in response to instructions or from a need for revenge, incomprehensibly draconian. But instead of rejoicing that finally one of these juridical monsters, who always talk their way out by saying that they had been forced to be inhuman, was hailed into court, my first thought was: But they pulled in none from among the Nazi judges, not a single one . . . I can't resist the thought—presumably because of my father's influence.

You can of course demand that a grown man not indulge in thinking of things without contradiction, but that's exactly where the problem lies: My father carried out his work so thoroughly that the first-mentioned thought seems to me, twenty-two years after his death, representative and appropriate. Why for anything in the world should I forget that in West Germany without exception all the Nazi judges got off unpunished, indeed, that most of them were not even forced to change their profession? And anyone who is upset by that, who asks: Why are you so severe this time, when before you showed such infinite generosity? will get as a reply: You're right, of course, but we don't want to make the same mistake a second time. And again my father forces me to think that this argument is mendacious and hypocritical, and that is connected not at all so secretly with what is taking place today on the streets of Germany.

Now and then I am occupied by the question about whether Max Becker in our days would have made the same choice of a place to live as after the war, whether I, too, under the same conditions would have become a German. I never tire of imagining myself as someone else, perhaps because it is a kind of occupational sickness to fumble around in stories and to invent them over and over. I know that until 1972, the year in which he died, my father never regretted his decision; he lived in East Berlin in surroundings in which, admittedly, he did not flourish, in which, however, it gradually stopped being important that he was a Jew. Actually he wasn't a Jew at all, that is, it wasn't important to him to be one. But he never concealed it. I even believe that often he made more of his Jewishness than was comfortable for him: out of fear of being considered conformist, thus out of pride. Once he said that never in his life would it have occurred to him to think of himself as a Jew, if there were no anti-Semites. Nothing in the world demanded the solidarity of Jews and their consciousness of their unique character as hatred of Jews. And concerning the GDR he said: The anti-Semites there were forced so expansively into denial, that it was possible to get along with them very well.

He died soon enough that he didn't have to recant. The results of unification would have hit him hard, of that I am convinced; he would soon have come to the end of his patience. If he had still had enough strength, he would probably have taken a globe one time or another and searched for a more pleasant place on earth. He would have said: 'I had a bad feeling from the start'—that's what he said every time when something unforeseen and at the same time unpleasant happened.

One can probably state that German unification was something unforeseen. I hope you don't consider it a painful admission if I say that I never longed for it. No wish of mine has been fulfilled, particularly not one I've held for a long time, how could it have taken possession of me? The two divided states were for me a kind of natural condition that corresponded to all of my experiences just as to my father's need for security. With amazement, when the Brandenburg Gate was opened, did I see the many tears of emotion, even in the eyes of people whom until then I had considered people like me. Unification is no one's gain, not something like the result of a clever, far-sighted policy that many, in hindsight, offer as their own. Rather it is the consequence of catastrophes, of mismanagement, of debacles. First the Soviet Union collapsed, then Eastern Europe, and almost at the end, my father's GDR. And that was the moment when nothing more was left for the ruling politicians than the attempt to put together what until this day won't fit together. What else were they supposed to do? Not bother with this matter?

For ages Germans have not been held to be a cheerful people. Anyone who sees them walking sombrely and worriedly along the streets can count on it that nothing special has happened. Since their unification, however, the country seems seized by an irritation that goes far beyond the customary measure, by a bad mood such as can be observed after important soccer games at which the wrong team won. Are people who have finally gotten their will supposed to be in such a mood? Is a family whose time of separation is finally past supposed to be so unhappy? Is a people for whom a dream has come true supposed to look like that?

I imagine how my father would have said: 'What do you care—let them be as grim as they want; the Germans have *their* problems, you have yours.' But suddenly I feel how his influence dwindles. In contrast to him I have acted for many years as though I belonged, so long that no other role is possible for me. He lived with the fiction that he had the free choice between this and all other countries, that the world belonged to him—an illusion that is not granted me. I definitely have no better country; I'd like to find out what is wrong with the only one I have. Stupidly I know already now that all my trouble will be in vain: either I will find out nothing, which is the most probable case; or on the other hand, even if I should succeed in hitting upon the traces of one explanation or another, not a single person will profit from it. We have been living, it seems to me, in a time when explanations lead to nothing. Analyses are of importance only when they concern technological processes, when economic interests come directly into play. But attempts to explain conditions in society are more and more a matter for hobbyists. The trend is all too clear: The well-being of our society comes before anything, and still it doesn't want to know where it stands. Diagnosticians are not forbidden to speak, but people turn away from them deathly bored. There is an epidemic of not wanting to now.

Not long ago an American acquaintance of mine told me that the East and West Germans couldn't endure one another, and he had a lot of understanding for both. I couldn't put up with that; I answered with something similar to—he was the one to talk, the Americans had already always been inclined to rash, superficial judgements. It was easier to make dumb jokes the less one paid attention to the facts. I knew many West and East Germans, I asserted, who had easily taken pleasure with one another: as an East German I had married a West German. I must admit that I didn't sound very convincing. I ran into a judgement that conforms to my own observations: East and West Germans don't like one another. Why?

The primary possible reason that comes to my mind: Perhaps it's a matter of resentments that East and West German come to feel in the other part of the country, respectively, of nothing other than hatred of foreigners, of a kind of enmity toward strangers that remains unrecognized because it apparently is directed to their own countrymen. Because that people who could not be more foreign to one another became a

citizens of a single country is something you can bet
on. You ought to be skeptical of the fairy tale about a
common background, common history, common culture. Isn't their background immaterial, their culture
tiresome, their history unknown to most citizens, here
as well as there? It can easily be maintained that
Hölderlin or the contest of minstrels at Wartburg or
the Hambach Fair united the people of Böblingen and
Cottbus; but for all practical purposes such a determination would have no correspondence in reality.
Perhaps East and West Germans will be incurable
strangers for one or two generations; just consider
that the line of separation that is so concisely called
the interior German border is basically the same border that, let's say, separated the Belgians from the
Mongolians. Purely and simply the border.

I don't want to dwell long on the reasons for the
mutual lack of liking one another that are so apparent
that anyone can see them. The different economic status is quite plain, and naturally that puts pressure on
the mood of all concerned: on those who are being
forced to relinquish more of their prosperity than they
consider justified as well as on those who believe that
they have a claim to a faster assimilation. Not a few
feel themselves patronized and colonized, principally,
to be sure, only in the East. Not a few feel themselves
drawn into a matter that looked at first like a popular
fair and that has meanwhile turned out to be wearily

and boringly and dangerously uncertain. Not a few, faced with the difficulties that grew like dandelions, found themselves longing for a past that never existed. In any event it would take faith in a miracle to expect that the prospects of the people would converge as long as the circumstances of their lives are so different. That existing determines consciousness, at least substantially, such a Marxist thesis was supposed to be allowed to continue in force. Only a comparable prosperity will converge the opinions of the East and the West (or a comparable state of emergency) and homogenize the country to a certain extent.

Colonization may be a too crass and emotional word, but I cannot conceal the fact that I don't consider the anger of many East Germans about patronization, disdain, being taken advantage of, tactlessness to have come out of thin air. An unspoken Western principle of unification was: Your regulations are no good, from now on ours count. Just about all East German norms were removed, not because they had proven to be the worse in individual cases but because they had been in force on the wrong side. Why must alcohol be allowed to be drunk before driving a car? Why are Communist anti-fascists less appropriate for street names than Prussian princesses? Why should sixty miles per hour be done away with, if not in the interest of environmental ruin and the auto industry? Why have the GDR pregnancy regulations been removed if not to increase the realm of

power of the Catholic Church? Why is the constitu-
tional decision *restitution before compensation* been
issued if not in the interest of a devastating restora-
tion? (As is heard from those who make decisions, it is
a matter of justice, but what kind of benefit is it when
in the interest of justice hundreds of thousands of
injustices are committed?) As a result of such a principle such horrible demands have been made and in part
fulfilled that hardly anyone would be astonished if the
successors of I. G. Farben were to announce their
claims for Auschwitz.

However correct or not the reasons mentioned
for German irritation may be—I consider another
more grave. In one part of the world, which called
itself with involuntary frankness the Socialist Camp, a
proud idea has been so discredited and destroyed that
none of us will experience the attempt to raise it up
again. Socialism is gone for the long haul, not in
books and discussions, but in so-called real life. What
was organized under the name of socialism has justi-
fiably foundered; and however much I would wish for
an honourable, successful attempt, far and wide I see
no society that would be prepared to surrender itself
for the next experiment. Appropriate personnel is
lacking, the party with the programme that enthuses
the masses as well as the masses themselves are lacking. Except that changes nothing in the fact that the
problems that the socialists vowed to solve will not
stop existing.

The capitalistic system is the victor. The Western way of living has proven to be the more effective and more stable and in the eyes of by far most people as the most desirable. The German states of the West are the homeland, the Eastern ones an amalgamated region. The citizens of the amalgamated region felt attracted irresistibly by the conditions in the homeland; all of them, almost all of them, wanted finally to live too like the others had been able to for a long time, encouraged by the mercy of the right occupation power. Forgotten the talk of the socialist conditions of production, of *each according to his ability, to each according to his accomplishments*, which was hypocrisy anyway. God knows there wasn't much to lose, and without long hesitation they submitted to the new principles. The difficulties in doing that were considered at first as start-up difficulties. I presume that a thought, a mean suspicion, was suppressed a millionfold: That the new, the Western ideals are wrong. That they are more suitable for an end than for a new beginning. Many people know that, therefore their discontent.

Anyone who asserts that the vitality of the GDR for at least forty years was explainable only with its apparatus of suppression is making a fool of himself. There was indeed a certain acceptance of Party views among the populace; less when it was a matter of the assessment of state achievements and accomplishments, more in appraisals of the West. Being forced to give up consumption, for example, promoted insight into the questionability of boundless consumption. The acknowledgement was anything but voluntary, as we have seen meanwhile—the fox had recognized that the unreachable grapes are too sour. But where is it written that such insights are correct, when they come into existence without force? And even when it's a matter of very scanty insights, even if they withstood the first real test of the burden, it existed nonetheless. And its memory is not completely erased.

The relative prosperity of the West has two pre-requisites: first, the ruthless, constantly increasing consumption of the resource called the future, second, the poverty of a great part of the population of the earth—a poverty that is connected with our wealth in a kind of linked conduits. Even if you ignore the moral aspect of such behaviour, even if you don't worry about the question of how long the starving will keep quiet and those cheated of their future will go still along, simple arithmetic shows that our happy consumption must be finite. It won't be all right very much longer, jobs are becoming scarce, security is get-ting scarce, water is getting scarce, air is getting scarce, a great, black misery is coming closer and closer, and nobody is standing in its way. We don't want to know anything about it, for meeting the danger means con-tinuing to live with enormous curtailments, and we're not ready for that. We can't get away from our ghoul-ish *business as usual*, we defame the few among us who warn us as starry-eyed alarmists, we think—it will be all right. But somehow, against our will, we know deep inside that the matter *can't* be all right. The more often our business freedom is disturbed— and the disturbances will never halt—such thoughts will burden us all the more. Another reason for the bad humour.

Don't underestimate the fact that the mere exis- tence of socialist countries represented hope in the eyes of many people. Moreover, with those who were not clear about that hope, even by many who lived in the West and considered the other side as opponents. I'm not at all certain whether their numbers decreased. The more socialist it became in the East, the clearer it became that absolutely nothing happened there with which hope could be linked. The very presence of two opposed political systems stimulated a contest for the more reasonable form of human life together that seemed to be like an assurance for the future. In order to survive the duel, in the long run they would have nothing remaining but to optimize their own forms of economizing and regulating—that was what they hoped. That in truth it was a matter of a contest of folly, eyes were shut for such an augury.

Now many realize that the contest is over, that they are being forced to do anything at all by no one except by their own good sense, and that there's no reliance on that. Consciousness of being left to their own devices is growing, and after all the experiences they have had, the worst can be feared. In the West the Easterners seem as a result to be not only people who, although one's own problems are large enough, must be grasped under the arms—they have deprived one of important hopes. You don't know how, you don't know by what means, you just feel it—they have. And that should not create discontent?

I consider the growth of extremism on the Right as *one* result of general bitterness. Some analysts of society, also colleagues of mine, believe they can explain the readiness of young people to set fire to houses of foreigners and foreigners themselves from a certain deficit of theory. One has withheld from these young people concepts such as fatherland, love for home, or national pride for too long, one has left them alone with their need for Germanness, one has barred them from an indispensable field of activity through useless taboos. One has driven them into an emotional trap in such a way that their outbreaks of violence were the logical result of that desiccation. Someone even said—cries for help. Such an explanation seems to me to be extremely odd, for it presumes that there is a natural, as it were an inborn, inclination for a great community; that therefore patriotism belongs to the basic make-up of a person.

I, on the other hand, suspect that we have to do with a way of behaviour that is produced by the condition of society described above, by anxiety about the future, loss of perspective, a mood of Armageddon. Of course, not all young people deduce the decision from that to join scrapping hordes, but the most primitive and intolerant and power-mad do just that. I consider it somewhat curious to impute to them a great regret about denied theories of whatever sort. And should there be a need for a different image of history, then it would be one for a distorted image of history, for an untruthful one. Is there a duty to accede to that?

Two problems should not be confused with one another: One is how we can prevent the transformation of young people into young Nazis, the other, how we should treat those in whom the change has already taken place. However important preventive measures are, I fear that the victims of the acts of violence do not have enough time to wait for their effects. It's easy to raise demands for better education, better housing, more jobs, except that we're a long way from having a better education, better housing, more jobs.

I hear from analysts, especially from one, that it is a fallacy to call groups who love violence, to whom many streets belong when it gets dark, Right extremists—in reality they merely want to break a taboo. Aside from the fact that doing so they break many bones, I find that it's not a fallacy at all. Not merely because they miss no opportunity to point to their closeness to the Nazi Party, SS and the like—with rituals, with kicks or with concise maxims that do not exceed their ability to comprehend them, but above all because intolerance, primitivism and violence belong to the fascist temperament.

How shall we treat them? With patience? With an indifference as with children whose behaviour does get on our nerves but whom we indulge because we've learned that they must outgrow certain basic needs? No, I think that's not right. I think there's not enough patience to last to the end of this violence. Besides it's not merely a matter of a pedagogical process, the matter is demanding human lives. And besides, for a long time patience has been practised by state's attorneys and judges who generally treat the delinquents in a way that make us have curious thoughts.

With more enlightenment? Yes, there can't be enough enlightenment, the end of enlightenment would be like the end of reason. But enlightenment has boundaries that cannot be moved by its own might. All delinquents encounter the most enlightened arguments on every street corner without allowing themselves to be led astray. Enlightenment absolutely, but what if efforts toward enlightenment are nothing but a joke to our rampaging young countrymen? It would be wonderful if everything depended on the right arguments; then the great age of the wise would begin.

Patience will get us nowhere, and enlightenment won't, what then? Perhaps more civil courage? Please

believe me that no one would be more delighted with
more civil courage than I, but is *that* to be the solution? A kind of individual armament against drinking,
brawling, violent criminals unwilling or unable to
think. Imagine, on every corner a little civil war
would be happening, in which now the good would
win, but mostly the wrong ones, for they are more
practised in those kinds of affairs. Imagine they
would start to look around for appropriate weapons;
for who can get used to being constantly slapped
around, especially when pride were not involved but
fear. I am convinced that such conditions would exert
a power of attraction even on persons who today
aren't members of the Party: who from a lack of
opportunity have to compensate for their aggressions
in bars, on sports spectators or in the family. Suddenly
there would be a wonderful field of action in every
neighbourhood.

Or does anyone hope that civil courage could
lead to the desired success in the perimeters of violence? If maybe skinheads thrash Vietnamese heads
with baseballs bats, does anyone hope that they
would think twice about their courageously spoken
statement? 'What you're doing there is contemptuous
of humans!'

The state's monopoly of violence is an indispensable civilized achievement, probably the most important in the history of humankind. It gives us the

possibility of climbing down from the trees without fear, to emerge from our caves and, finally liberated by the club in our hands, to go about our business. It gives us the possibility of carrying out our differences of opinion, even when our opponent is a head taller or when the group of opponents is stronger than we. The consistency with which the monopoly of violence is carried through stands in direct relationship to the fear with which or without which we live. The more we rely on the fact that the state protects us from violence (most practicable also its own), all the more do we respect it. Indeed, it is exactly the deepest sense of its existence to spare us physical self-defence. Not only because we aren't suited for that because we're always inferior to the use of violence by specialized groups but also because it would look ominous for a state whose well-being might depend on the civil courage of its citizens.

The demand of agencies, of police and courts, to kindly do their work should not be confused with the so-called call for a strong state. Much more important as a drastic measure for me would be the certainty that I had to do with a state that in this matter at least stands on my side. That it's the sincere need of state attorneys, leaders of special forces, government bureaucrats to get control of the violent Rightist extremists. I'm far away from that certainty. On television I see police raids in which attacks are made on youthful, whistling demonstrators against the economic conference, but never on demonstrating neo-Nazis who yell 'Heil Hitler!' and wave flags and leave behind a trace of devastation. By the way, the following practice has meanwhile been established: A Right extremist party or group applies to hold a demonstration, whereupon a Leftist group applies for a counter demonstration, whereupon both demonstrations are prohibited, whereupon the Rightists complain about the prohibition, whereupon in a short time the complaint is granted but the counter demonstration remains prohibited, whereupon the Leftist group demonstrates anyway, whereupon the police force acts exclusively against the Leftist group, strictly according to the law.

I see government politicians turn away from the camera when it's a matter of taking a position about the outbreaks of hate. Hardly does a foreigner's house burn than the Federal Chancellor has his speakers proclaim that the terror by the Left and the Right must be stopped, almost always in that sequence, and always without having any kind of action follow one half of the announcement. You must understand that one party would not like a growing part of its constituents to be offended; but if it wishes to remain electable at any price for Rightist extremists, then probably the conclusion is not exaggerated that it supports Right extremism.

Presumably you know the results of polls according to which twenty per cent of Germans admit openly to being anti-Semitic and only thirty per cent are so-called opportunistic anti-Semites. I myself receive letters that I won't spread out before you, but which aren't exactly friendly. I know from a television editor that after broadcasts that are about the persecution of Jews, letters are written by viewers in which the wildest anti-Semitic epigrammatic statements are found, letters that come from East as well as West Germany and are by no means anonymous—a development that was unthinkable even a few years ago. After the synagogue in Lübeck was set afire recently, Foreign Minister Kinkel said in an interview: 'Arsons like the one in Lübeck awaken the impression abroad as though there were in Germany a broad anti-Semitic movement.'

That sounds not only remarkably unsuspecting and nonsensical, the statement is also treacherous. The Foreign Minister's concern applies not to German conditions, it applies to the image that Germany offers. What will they think of us, how are we doing? But strictly speaking, it isn't also concern for our reputation that moves our Foreign Minister, rather it is fear that business could get worse. Such a fear wouldn't be unjustified: Deliberations are underway everywhere about whether goods must be bought necessarily from a country in which almost daily houses of foreigners burn; in which television commentators say that the background of the act is still unclear; in which those who seek asylum are spat upon so often that it is hardly worth reporting anymore; in which agitators are allowed to call those who warn against them agitators without a court being prepared to take action against them; in which a neo-Nazi says at meetings that the Jews themselves had spread the fairy tale of the slaughter of Jews throughout the world in order to defame Germany; in which the federal court as the court of highest jurisdiction steps in protectively before this man and turns over his conviction by a lower court. Our balance of trade is already feeling the effects, and if you ask me—I put certain hopes in that. The pressure that is created in this way could replace discernments and lead to a breath of determination.

Whenever I ask myself where the heavily prejudiced aversion to thinking, where the stupidity, where the lust for violence in so many people come from, especially in so many young people, I am somewhat at a loss. I do not trust the explanation that social complications are chiefly responsible. Of course, there are all the more gangsters in a society where the discrepancy between material desires and the possibility to satisfy them exists. Obviously unemployment, loss of physical well-being, hopelessness and homelessness have an effect. Nevertheless, I do not believe that such disadvantages, let's call them poverty in sum, predestine a young man to knock foreigners to pieces. We're not dealing here simply with gangsters; it's the Nazi parts involved that are so scary. Why is a great part of the violence directed against Angolans and synagogues and gravestones and Turks, against victims from whom *nothing* can be gained? It is evident that an out-and-out piece of fascism has survived in Germany. How was that possible?

As far as West Germany is concerned, I am inclined to follow the simple theory of my father: The survival took place in the most natural way, in the forms of persons. In the form of businessmen, officers, jurists, widows, teachers, bankers, state secretaries, journalists, churchmen—the list is anything but complete. Most of them are dead, but their traces cannot be overlooked. By no means did they appear from the first minute after the war on as incorrigible Nazis—first of all, that wouldn't have been very clever, second the Allies would have prohibited it. I don't even want to exclude the fact that many of them for a short time were crippled by a bad conscience or by a trace of regret. But whatever their state of mind may have been, they determined the atmosphere in the Federal Republic substantially, to this very day. They saw to it that the look back at the Nazi past turned out as mild as possible, not brutal, and where it was possible they tried to prevent it. They never grew weary of warning against self-abasement, dirtying their own nests, self-laceration. They appeased, smoothed over, transfigured, pointed at the injustice of others. They prevented punishments from taking place, they succeeded in getting sentences suspended. They supported one another mutually and supplied influence for one another. They prevented the progress of those who had seen through them. They said that not *everything* had been bad in those days, you couldn't throw out the baby with the bath water. Some time or other they got the idea of asserting that fascism had simply been the answer to the *real* crime of our epoch, to Bolshevism. They said—some time or other there must be an end.

In the GDR the situation was different. There the Nazi ideas that have very recently become visible survived not in the form of people who little by little occupied positions—they were hardly there. That must be explained: After the war a small migration of peoples took place in Germany. The more Nazi he was, the more exposed he was, the more compromised he was, then the more likely did he move from East to West. It was clear to him that he had more to fear from the Russians than from the Americans: not because they were the more brutal fellows, but because he had done more to them. The Americans, the chief among the Western Allies, radiated the laxity of victors, the Russians were beside themselves. So the Soviet Union indirectly shares the responsibility for the West German Nazi density being considerably larger than the East German one. But at least in this regard the relationships in the whole country have adapted. With something like experimental proof, we observe that the Nazi temperament must not absolutely be transmitted from mouth to mouth, rather that it can come into existence anew, even though not out of a void.

From its first hour on, the GDR lived with a lie. It invented a history for itself that never took place— its forefathers were said to be the German anti-fascists. Beyond that there was no earlier. Naturally the crimes of the Nazis were discussed, even extraordinarily so, but those were the crimes of others. Fascism had nothing to do with us, the people in the GDR; in a miraculous way we had rid ourselves of the facts. Films about the Nazi time were always films about the anti-fascist resistance; school instruction about the Nazi time was not instruction about our earliest history, it always concerned the misdeeds of those terrible *aliens* whom we, the anti-fascists, with some support by the Red Army, had vanquished. Of the ten thousand anti-fascists who may have been in Nazi Germany, merely eight million lived in the GDR.

Since we, the people of the GDR, never indulged in the *self*-criticism of our past, our glance at the fascist-like in our own circumstances and in our own behaviour was lost. Whenever our society was called intolerant or violent, we dismissed it as hostile defamation; in our own country such statements were prosecuted. We could not or didn't want to see how filled to the brim by untruthfulness and shamelessness and hostility to foreigners and a spirit of submission and denunciation and injustice—daily profound injustice—our own country was. Statements that sounded friendly to fascism were strictly prohibited; ways of behaviour that resembled fascism were commonplace: that one Party without exception had to determine everything, that we had to cheer it whenever it was concerned; that which films were allowed to be shown and which books printed and which houses built depended on the taste of its limited leadership; that small children had to wear red cloths around their necks and at the press of a button had to shout 'always prepared'; that informers were sitting everywhere who handed on every suspicious word simply because they had to be afraid of being spied on themselves; that anyone who tried to flee these circumstances risked his life and that, if he wasn't shot but was taken to court, he was called an enemy *of the people*. All of that did not smack of fascism?

It would be dishonest to maintain that only through the fall of the Wall could the bacillus have spread into the adjoining area. The Western Nazis were probably better organized, and they understood more about public work, but with that they also exhausted their advantage. German unification was, in any event, also the unification of the potential with the already practising Rightist radicals.

The newly established formation is incalculable; it frightens many, to many its nothing but embarrassing, it hardly bothers most. To me it seems as though the matter is followed with more attention abroad, as though the worry there were greater. My aforementioned American acquaintance said that the domestic reactions seemed to him to be curiously apathetical, apathetical and halfhearted. I don't want to contradict him. But he also said consolingly, all over the world people seemed to be more and more hesitant in solving their problems—they were surrounded by so many perils, that they just had no idea with which one to start. Possibly that was also the case with Germany.

I know that it is customary to conclude speeches with a reference to better prospects, at least with an indication of hope. I'm sorry that I'm unable to follow that practice. The most optimistic thing that comes to my mind to say is: Maybe we Germans will succeed in not arriving at the abyss earlier than most of the others. This task is anything but a child's game, but I don't consider it insoluble.

Translated by A. Leslie Willson

With this lecture I am participating in a project that I am not quite comfortable with and whose worth has yet to be proven. Before I began writing this lecture, I had to decide between one of two possibilities: I could either tell you why, despite my reservations, I am taking part, or I could state the reasons for my uneasiness. I chose the second option. It seems to me to be slightly more illuminating. But there is definitely something strange about a lecture that consists mainly of a list of reasons why it should not have been presented.

My first concern stems from an unwillingness to talk about myself. Please don't confuse this with modesty; it has more to do with a well-grounded fear. It does not become anyone to explain to an audience how lacking and superficial his knowledge of himself is. Whenever I have attempted to examine the influences of earlier experiences on my present actions, I have failed. Either I became bored unusually quickly, and then floundered around in a wave of assumptions and stopped my self-analysis short, before anything was revealed, or I was overcome with angst: I said to myself, until now things have gone fairly well, so my knowledge of myself must be sufficient; if I pursued this, I would just end up disturbing the peace of mind I should be happy about.

Or I thought, there's absolutely nothing to find out; I don't need to look for secrets where there aren't any. I am a child of Jewish parents; my native tongue is Polish. I survived a ghetto and two concentration camps; don't ask me how. Only after the war did I come to Germany, learn German, and become a German. That is all relatively clear. After almost fifty years I am still not rid of the feeling of being a stranger in my new environment. At first I wanted to overcome this feeling as soon as possible; in the meantime I've become used to it and would probably be scared to death if I were to wake up one morning and this feeling were no longer there. In my work I sporadically deal with Jewish matters, in the past more so than now. I never deal with Polish matters; I'm not familiar with them—I only lived in a Polish environment as a child. I have forgotten everything that ever had to do with Poland, and my father, the only one who could have prevented this, never felt like a Pole and was not very fond of Poland. What is there in all this to analyse?

The second reason for my hesitation has to do with a lack of desire to invest time in projects that, with great probability, will not lead to anything. It's a question of dexterity to agree with any arbitrary outcome of such a venture and to arrive at this point via a fairly elegant path. I'm afraid I have this dexterity. I would be capable of portraying myself as one in whose texts this and that influence is present, whose biography has this and that consequence for his writing, whose confused cultural identity can be found in this and that way in his books. But that would be pure charlatanism, because the truth is, I know virtually nothing about all this.

In the twenty-five years that I have been a writer, I have often read how critics or Germanists have done with my texts precisely what I now refuse to do (out of coyness, some of you may say), and this has not always seemed futile to me. But there is a difference whether the research is done with a certain distance from the object under scrutiny, with tools which are specifically made and tested for such research, or whether the examiner is himself the one to be examined—with his blinders, his vanity, his preference for a certain result. Besides that, he is better able to deal with the outsider's diagnosis; he can accept it or can disregard it as ridiculous. But it is impossible for him to find his own diagnosis ridiculous. He has to live with it.

It would be tedious if I wanted to replace my own work with a list of the so-called multicultural aspects that others have found or have wanted to find in my books. Most of that can be recognized immediately, and it is hardly enlightening to speak about the obvious. Believe me, I consider critics and Germanists more competent to comment on an author's work than the author himself. At least that is the usual case, because without a doubt ornithologists know more about the essence of birds than do the birds themselves. Nevertheless—and I hope this is not a sign of narrow-mindedness—I admit that no such analysis has ever really provoked me. I don't mean the type of provocation by which successful sentences or astonishing conclusions can help the reader. Rather, I mean the shiver that runs down your back when a secret is revealed in which you yourself are involved. No, I have never been so lucky. It was only what I already knew or guessed, oftentimes more precisely worded than I could have ever done, often in embarrassing clarity, but it was never a revelation. Please don't mistake this for a complaint or a reproach; perhaps I simply had false hopes. In any case, my conviction grew that literary criticism and literary theory constitute a genre, and that critics and scholars do nothing more than tell stories—a certain type of story, of course, as is appropriate to the genre, stories that fail as often or succeed as seldom as poems or novels.

Third, I must admit I suffer from a certain sense of modesty. I imagine that by explaining the idiosyncrasies of my own texts to you, I am in danger of behaving like an actor on a runway: my stomach held in, my chest thrust forward, and a far from charming smile on my face. Just look at these muscles, aren't they impressive? Please don't look at the layers of fat; I love to eat, as a result of my years as a ghetto child. . . . And if you'll cast a friendly glance at this scar— it's from an accident which happened as follows . . .

I imagine it would be an embarrassing performance for all involved, at which not even the voyeurs would be amused. And the reverse would also be unsightly, if I indulged in the other extreme in order to escape the sin of vanity: instead of holding in my stomach, I stick it out on purpose; in place of the superficial smile, affected seriousness. The effort to look natural would be in vain, I'm sure. It would only be successful if I ignored outer appearances and presented my text without frills. But I am not familiar with this, and as a result the frills would be my only salvation.

I don't want to say that it is an enviable situation, to know nothing about yourself. But the advantage of knowledge is not knowledge; increasing awareness should lead to increasing competence. I am not very hopeful, at least not with the topic we are discussing today. Rather, I fear impediment.

My work consists mainly of deciding what I consider worth telling, and then, after I've made this decision, of finding the right words. It is not always as systematic as it sounds: sometimes there is a word, or a few words, and then I have no idea what they are good for. I just like the way they stand there in their splendour, and I don't want to throw them away, out of stinginess, fear or lack of imagination; and somehow I have to give the impression that they belong. Yes, unfortunately that happens; actually, it is the norm. So, what I initially considered worthy of telling wants to run in all directions, constantly changing itself and offering new challenges, and I have to hold it together (which usually doesn't work) so that at the end it still has a hint of similarity to the original plan. I don't want to complain, but it is not a very easy task.

I have pointed out that at the beginning of a book (or story, or essay) the decision must be made: I, the author, consider this and that appropriate to be narrated. Now it might be understandable that the author will be asked why exactly he considers this and that worthy of being told, even if it is as equally understandable that the author does not want to talk about it (because he doesn't actually know, or because he is unsure, or because he indeed likes his story but finds the theory of this story lacking, or because it is embarrassing to explain oneself, or because it's nobody's business). Let's assume the conversation takes place, and let's assume the author says: 'I wrote *The Boxer* because I wanted to demonstrate that a Jew who has been freed from a concentration camp is a long way from being free. He has suffered deformations that do not disappear overnight and, yes, might never be overcome. I wanted to show that he has become unsuitable as a father, as an employee, as a husband, and to a certain extent as a citizen; and I wanted to show this with sympathy for him. I wanted to express the idea that such a person deserves our sympathy, but that he has no right to be above criticism. I thought, if someone in Germany should write about this, then preferably me rather than a normal German.' (By the way, that would be information that would turn my stomach, but luckily it is only hypothetical.)

Let's assume that the author has a friendly disposition, is communicative and open. However, that does not help him much, because after he has talked himself blue, in the manner described, after he has overcome his inhibitions and tried to substantiate the insufficient reasons for his decision, he is asked the next question: 'Do you believe that certain circumstances in your biography are responsible for this decision and not another?'

No later than here—and I find myself approximately at this point—the alarming thought arises: 'Protect yourself, they'll have your head!' That is definitely a bit exaggerated; certain circumstances in my biography are probably responsible for these panic attacks, but I don't want to go into that now. I say to myself: why do they want to know this? Above all I think: why do *I* have to know this? I am reminded of a fable—by the Russian poet Krylov, if I'm not mistaken—that I read as a child:

A centipede takes a walk in the woods and encounters a snail. The snail imagines she has never before seen such a graceful and beautiful creature. She immediately falls in love. She adores him and says, 'My God, how gracefully you move! You have such an infinite number of legs that one would think you'd be tripping all the time. And yet you never get mixed up, all your movements are completely coordinated. Tell me your secret—how do you accomplish such a masterpiece?' The centipede is extremely flattered—for what centipede is used to such high praise? Blushing, he smiles at the snail and says, 'I'm so glad you like the way I walk! You know, it's not so easy to answer your question, because, to tell you the truth, I've never thought about it. Wait a minute.' And making up for lost time, he begins to ponder the secret of his movement. He thinks and thinks and thinks. The fable, as you can probably imagine, ends with the sentence, 'And from this moment on he could no longer walk.'

Once I heard a writer talk about himself, as listeners asked him questions at a public reading of his

work. He had none of my winsome scruples. He willingly provided every last bit of information and
appeared to be quite at ease in doing so. When asked
about his image of women, he said his mother died
young and his father's second wife was often cool and
indifferent toward him. He was never able to understand what his father saw in her. As a child he never
knew any caring, kindhearted women, and it would
border on a miracle if this were to have no effect on
his books. When asked why his books are so often set
in foreign lands, he said that ever since his childhood
he has suffered from a desire to travel. He constantly
went to the circus, where the artists' tricks were less
interesting than the circus wagons, where different
languages were spoken and scents from foreign lands
filled the air. His favourite subject in school was geog-
raphy. When asked which authors had influenced
him, he named four without hesitation: Hermann
Hesse, Karl May, and two others I had never heard of
and therefore forgot. In any case they seemed to be
two exotic authors.

I was surprised that my colleague was so willing
to reveal so much about himself, how he knew everything about himself and did not hesitate to let anyone
who so desired take part in his intimate thoughts. But
I cannot say that I got any closer to him that evening,
even though I was given information unknown to me
previously.

Until now I have been unwilling to speak about aspects of my texts that one could say are determined by my Jewishness and about those that do not necessarily have to do with my Polish heritage but perhaps with an affinity to Eastern European culture which results from this heritage. Recently a new identity among my identities has suddenly surfaced: the East German. Yes, I call this a culturally relevant influence: to be a German writer with three-quarters of an East German life behind him. It would be easiest for me to speak about the consequences of this biographical period, for here I don't feel as strongly the inhibitions I just mentioned, but rather a tinge of necessity. Perhaps this is because it is so close to me without haunting me, or because I am so aware of its influences that one could call these influences a theme, or because, even though remembering this past involves hundreds of discomforts, it is not a trauma.

Of course I will not begin now to examine how and where East Germany has revealed itself in my books. It would devalue my other origins if I were to place this particular one, the most recent and most obvious of them, in the foreground. To be quite honest, this part of my constitution is the least pleasing to me—and that is reason enough not to make such a fuss about it. Usually I don't like it when I recognize traits in me that can be considered East German, and I say to myself, 'You should pay more attention to that the next time.' On the other hand, I don't mind—or, in the least advantageous case, care—if I act in a way which others call Jewish. I react infinitely more harshly and more aggressively to verbal discrimination against Jews than against East Germans, and not because I find it more dangerous (which it undoubtedly is) but rather because it seems more scandalous.

Even though I have written several articles and given several speeches about how many injustices the East Germans have had to deal with during the unification of Germany, I often have to suppress the thought: 'But to some extent they also deserved it.' Or even worse: 'To some extent we deserved it.'

Since I left the GDR eighteen years ago and moved to the West, I have succeeded in whitewashing the fact that in reality I belong to the losing side of unification. If an actor leaves the stage and the play goes on without him, does he escape responsibility for the quality of the whole piece? I, however, hang around with the winners, drink with them, tell jokes with them and enjoy the same comforts. Now and again acquaintances of old, East Germans, come to me and ask for advice: 'Tell us, how did you manage to become one of them? Share a few tricks with us?' Then I shrug my shoulders or rattle off a few phrases which no one knows what to do with, especially not the people asking; and then they leave with one less hope and say behind my back that I used to show more solidarity, that I've been on the other side too long.

I don't know if they are right; maybe a little. I try not to dwell too long on this question. I say to myself, it's not of great importance. As they leave, I am capable of so little empathy that it surprises me; after all, I have never considered myself heartless. I used to be one of them, I think, and I am happy that it's all behind me. But later, when I'm sitting at my desk, it's a long way from being behind me. It's an uncomfortable feeling that you can belong to those you would rather be done with.

And finally, the last reason I prefer to keep quiet about the multiculturally determined particles of my texts lies far from all modesty or airs. I sense that when books are multiculturally inspired, it is a defect which can scarcely be repaired. In other words, I prefer monocultural books, the more monocultural the better. The narrower the horizon they try to lead me to, the more willing I am to follow. I know this needs to be explained. But if you could be patient for a minute and accept that this is really my opinion, as mixed up as it may seem to you, then the cause of my hesitation will become understandable. By speaking about the multicultural aspects of my own stories, I would be giving a lecture about their weaknesses. Without a doubt there are plenty of weaknesses, but why for heaven's sake should I be the one to do this?

I hope you don't regard my statement as praise of narrow-mindedness and bias, because what I want from individual books would be totally ridiculous when demanded of all the literature of one country. Each country's literature should show interest in world matters; there should be room for the most unique forms, opinions and prejudices; it should benefit from all of humanity's knowledge. Crossing over and mastering a foreign culture—or, should we say, one other than your own—is like gaining the ability to see the world with other eyes. This applies to everyone, and thus of course to people who write.

If authors are multiculturally influenced and this multiculturalism plays a role in their books without their realizing it, without their being able to defend themselves against it, and without their striving for it, then there is nothing to be said against this. If, however, the book is a result of a multiculturally composed endeavour—that is, if the writer is a dogooder who wants to bring the colours of the world to light in his book—then this method is questionable. I imagine the author who steps back from his work like a painter, critically examining it and arriving at the conclusion: I've done well with the Southern European part, but perhaps I need a few more dashes of Iberian-American mysticism to help matters. That might sound exaggerated and flippant, but all I wish to say is that the author who tries to become master over his various secrets will suffer defeat.

I know a colleague who, with all his energy, including that reserved for writing, has pursued one main concern for years: improving the situation of asylum-seekers in Germany. Unremittingly he meets with many of these pitiable people, deals with their problems, asks about their concerns, travels to their homelands, reads their literature and strives to understand their customs. His stories deal with hardly anything else, but not even the most well-intentioned and risk-taking publisher will print them, because their weaknesses are evident almost at first glance. The stories are like travelogues on foreign cultures. They are like collection plates offered to the reader so that he can donate his sympathy; but there is nothing tempting about these stories, nothing seductive.

There might have been authors who, like higher powers, were not bound by gravity, who hovered above the commonplace and could write as if the whole world were their district. Goethe perhaps, Voltaire perhaps, perhaps Joyce, whose setting was called Dublin but whose territory was the universe. Their points of reference were so vastly diverse and so unparalleled in their totality that it would be ridiculous to call them proof of how writers are able to bring the most diverse influences under one roof.

Hardly anyone would maintain that a prominent characteristic of writers like Dostoevsky or Hamsun or Faulkner was that they were multiculturally inspired.

Nevertheless, it appears to me that they, much more so than the previously mentioned authors, represent the relationship of a literary work to its roots, as found in thousands of other works, as is—please excuse the use of this word in this context—normal. Although they cannot be counted among the rank and file of literature, they do resemble us, the normal writers, at least in this one point. They wrote what they had to write; the influences of their environment were extremely important to them; the events of the world at large appeared in their books only to the extent that they had meaning for the events in their own street.

I love provincial writers: who are plagued by nothing so much as by the happenings in the village and on the few neighbouring farms; who are so taken by these events that they rarely reach the county seat, although they keep meaning to; who know every stone in their neighbourhood and every shortcut and every hiding place; who when writing have one language and when chatting with the neighbours have another without ever needing to put on airs or strike a pose; whose father and grandfather come from the village and whose mother at most comes from the neighbouring village, so that the story of the region and the story of their family can hardly be distinguished from each other; who know and describe the villagers' obsessions but who themselves also suffer from obsessions, without knowing about them; who, if fate throws them to unknown places, are driven to think and talk about their village, so much that the others consider them eccentric; who never aspire to be observers and reporters of our planet and, perhaps for this very reason, are.

Translated by Robert Rockwell and Jane Sokolosky

IT IS LIKE A THUNDERSTORM

Herlinde Koelbl in conversation with Jurek Becker

HERLINDE KOELBL: *Mr Becker, your novel* Jacob the Liar *is your biggest success to date. What do you think of your debut now, some twenty-eight years later?*

JUREK BECKER: You see, *Jacob the Liar* was my first book—in a way I wrote it before I was a writer. A first novel is always written by someone who is not yet a writer. If it goes well, he is one afterwards. And if it doesn't, he still isn't one. I am aware that *Jacob the Liar* is still my most popular novel. The book was a great blessing for me. It was so successful and it made my life as a writer very comfortable. After writing it I had opportunities I would not have had, had it been a flop. Nevertheless, I have a lot of issues with this book.

How come?

It seems linguistically premature to me. It is a well-designed book and it is—how shall I say it—pretty cleverly conceived. I still believe that today. It is a book that knows how to play with emotions. This is what I still admire about it, if I am even allowed to say these things about my own novel. But I also find it full of linguistic sloppiness, which I would not let myself get away with today. Unfortunately it was written in the GDR—and I didn't trust the publisher who released it there.

What does the one have to do with the other?

I did not trust the publishing company at all and I was always convinced that, when they criticized me, they actually meant something else. I thought every critique of the text was a political one and I kind of closed myself off to their suggestions. As a consequence, I didn't heed any editor's advice, even though it was a novel written by an amateur, which I was back then. So it is basically an unedited book. Which, with the wisdom of hindsight, I do not consider to be an advantage. I wish that the book could be carefully edited. But what am I supposed to do? *Jacob* is a good horse, so to speak, he just escaped before I could close the barn door.

It is still a novel that tells a wonderful story: The liar as the true hero. The story is the important thing, the language . . .

. . . is just tagging along.

In any event the language is very lively—whereas today your style is much more chiselled, more concise.

You are absolutely right. When I write, I would never think of considering what is in demand or what is standard or what expectations I have to fulfil. Rather, I try to approximate my own ideas of literature, no matter how right or wrong they may be. I believe there are no right or wrong ideas. It is about preferences, it is an affinity, and I am persistent in my attempt to adhere to my ideas. And maybe that is just what you read in *Jacob*, an image of what I used to be. And when you read my more recent texts, you get a more accurate image of what I am now. In the meantime, I have also read books which I hadn't read then and which have made a great impression on me.

Which books?

I believe, for example, that Arno Schmidt changed my writing, whether I like it or not. That Arno Schmidt helped me—how shall I say this—take a new look at the logic of writing, one that did not exist for me before. I believe that concerning myself with Kafka's works had consequences for me, even though I can't quite tell you what these consequences are.

You grew up in the Ghetto. This must surely have had an influence on you as well?

I can't say. A psychiatrist would have to find that out. I have no memories of it whatsoever. I can't tell you anything about the Ghetto. I forgot about it—it is as if it never happened.

Seriously?

As far as my memories are concerned, yes! Certainly not when it comes to my attitudes or a certain aggressiveness or . . . I really cannot make a judgement about this. The influence the Ghetto and the concentration camps had on me is unconscious, so I cannot talk about it. And I never tried to make it conscious— that is to say, I tried but I never had any success and, finally, I just stopped trying. I notice, for example, this is a piece of conclusive evidence, that there must be some influence, because I have such an interest in the topic and it's not like that's God-given. I notice that there is something obsessive there and that there is something that I am trying to figure out as a writer, and that must have something to do with my past. But I cannot tell you what it is.

Is it possible that, to some extent, you wanted to forget certain things because you needed to protect yourself?

I do not think that is the case with me. I don't think it has to do with repression and much less with some sort of desire to repress. I was curious pretty early on actually. I pestered my father, who lived until 1973, to talk to me about that time. He never wanted to. I never found out why. He closed himself off to these discussions. The first time I really devoted myself to the topic was when I wanted to write about it and started doing research. I went to archives, talked to so-called contemporary witnesses, none of whom I knew personally. Of those I knew, hardly anyone would talk to me about it. That's how it was.

But Jacob the Liar *is about life in the Ghetto, isn't it?*

Yes, yes, *Jacob* is in a way about: Where do you come from? Where do I come from? You know, I was like some kind of Kaspar Hauser who fell into the world at the age of eight. And, except for a few scant facts, nobody told me who I am and what is up with me and where I come from. And, for sure, *Jacob the Liar* was, in a sense, my attempt to piece together my autobiography. I wanted to know more about some things. What kind of a thing the Ghetto is I obviously knew much better afterwards than I did before. Before, the Ghetto was always this unsettling, menacing, black thing in my head. And I studied it until it became a place where people lived, people of whom I surely was one. I just don't know which one. I once wrote: If you don't know where you are from, it is a little bit like walking around all your life with a backpack on your back, a heavy bag, and you don't know what is inside. It is a very unpleasant state and dealing with it is almost a lifetime task—the effort to find out what is inside this damned backpack I am carrying.

The writer García Márquez said that he writes to be loved.

I don't think that is my reason for writing. Of course, I enjoy my books being liked. However, I do no more to achieve this than writing exactly the way I consider to be right. Oh I could think of ways—if I pursued them, my books would be liked by many more people than they are today. I am quite sure of that.

Does a book have to tell an authentic story in order to have appeal?

Hell no! You are not seriously going to tell me that Konsalik's books are authentic. Still they are embraced in a way that spooks me, that is crazy. Maybe I am a bit like García Márquez. Maybe I desire to be loved. My experience is that, when I write, a lot of people listen to me. That is pleasant. Maybe writing puts me at centre stage—something I never would have experienced otherwise. Maybe I just found out that I am quite good at this. And I realized that, at my desk, I can fly a little bit. Sometimes I read my own texts and I think, these texts are actually more intelligent than I am. And I ask myself how that is possible—I wrote them myself, there was no third party involved. This brings me to the conclusion that sometimes, but not always, I am able to do things at my desk that I would not be able to do otherwise, things I wouldn't be able to achieve in a conversation or with my actions, things I only succeed in during the act of 'writing'. I cannot think of any other motives for writing. Except for—excuse me—one other important thing: When you decide to become a writer, you also decide that writing is what you and your family are going to make a living off of. To make a living is a very important motive that drives me to write. And I would be a fraud to claim that this aspect of the matter does not play a role. If five novels of mine consecutively flopped, I would have to think of something.

Concerning your family: You are older now and you have recently become a father again. How does it feel to be a parent again at your age?

First of all, a child works as a perfect antidepressant. Secondly, and what I am telling you now is not just funny, I have two adult sons and my youngest son is six. The other two are thirty-five and thirty-two. And since my youngest son was born, I have the feeling that the other two, the older ones, grew up behind my back and I never really realized it. Now I know more. Of course, in retrospect, I feel sorry, but there is no way to change it now. You know, back then—I am talking about the time around thirty years ago now—if I was writing and the two came into my study, I would have surely kicked them out. It's clear, dad has got to write. I didn't need a better reason than that. Today, when my son disturbs me while I am working, I feel like I can't just throw him out. Somehow I start thinking: Someday, all of a sudden, he'll be sixteen and you won't even have noticed. That means I am more patient with him than I used to be, I am more curious than I used to be—and not so much for philanthropic reasons, not just because I decided to be a nice dad. There is some egotism to it. I get something out of it. I am having fun. And then I notice how all the old geezers my age envy me and that's fun too.

The decision to become a father again at this age— was it easy for you?

Oh I struggled like a madman. I saw hell coming right at me. I knew that this wasn't the way God had imagined it, that he had only created our nerves to last for so long before they reach their breaking point, but I was forced. My wife would not have married me otherwise and that's just how it is. A loaded gun was put to my chest and, in those moments, you don't have much of a choice other than being coerced into your own happiness.

But you took the risk. That's the crucial thing.

You are right and I do give myself credit for that. I know two people who were in a similar situation and decided differently. And sometimes it fills me with great satisfaction to look into their envious faces. We, my wife and I, realized that this child is everything but a pain. He is more like a little stove where we can go to warm ourselves. That is a great thing in our life.

Your wife is twenty-two years younger than you. Do you sometimes think about the many years of your child's life you won't live to see? The older you get . . .

Of course I think about that. That's just logical. I can't just cut off my imagination at a certain point. But thinking about something is different from worrying about it. It is the way it is and to lament the unchangeable is quite pointless. I'll tell you again: My two older sons had a father appropriate for their age and they didn't see much of me. And the little one has a father who is much older, but he gets to spend a lot of time with me. It's a kind of poetic justice. He might not have as many years with me though, I don't know. But tell me about a situation where you have as much of everything as you would like?

You are ill now and I'm sure it has been a tough time for you, a time of many struggles. To what extent has your experience of the radical limitedness of life influenced your writing?

I can't tell you. I do not know how it has influenced my writing. The only thing I can say is that I have always been conscious of not being immortal. Maybe it has become a bit more explicit now, but I am not aware that it has profoundly changed my relationship to my work.

Has your life changed?

Stupidly enough, just in detail. Going up stairs has become quite arduous, for example. Those kind of things. But apart from that, no. I just try, how shall I say this, to go about my business as usual.

Has being told that you have cancer thrown you off course?

Well I wasn't pleased to hear it. Everything that you really, really don't want to hear, when you hear it, results in some sort of concussion. That's the word for it. But I can't say I panicked. That's more my wife. I always try to tell her that it's all nature.

Not a great comfort.

You know, I'm not one of those people who constantly think about and poke around in things they cannot change. If thinking or immersing myself into the matter had any chance of success, if it would improve my chances of getting better, oh, you should see me think! But I try to keep this stuff as far away from me as possible. Not because I feel the need to repress it, I know what's going on—it's just that I can't see how it would bring any kind of relief if I were to let it get to me. And my wife is amazed at how I try and act as if there was nothing wrong. And I think it's the smartest thing to do.

Which means it's not a role that you're struggling to play, but real.

Oh yes. It's not like I have to pull myself together every morning, not at all. I am the same guy I've always been and every now and then the necessities entailed by this kind of illness catch up with me and I have to put up with them, whether I want to or not:

therapies, consultations, medication, all that is incredibly obnoxious. But, you know, I have no choice. It is like rain, it is like a thunderstorm, it's nature.

But don't you find nature to be exceptionally cruel and hard?

Of course I do. I just don't want to say to myself, oh my God, how awful. To be honest, I don't think that way. I'm not being coy when I say this, but I don't think I ever took my self too seriously. I was, let's say, intellectually ambitious, but I never believed that the world would not go on without me. I never thought that I was the essential brick in the wall, the brick that, if it's torn out, the wall collapses. On the contrary, whenever I noticed just how often others took themselves so seriously, it really bothered me. And maybe now this attitude is actually an advantage. My general disposition is: God, don't make such a fuss.

But now, when you see your little one all full of life and energy, doesn't it just break your heart?

Maybe yours, but not mine.

You have to think about it—

—No, no—

—because you know you will not be able to be with him for as long as he needs you or as long as you want?

Yeah, right, right. It sucks. It's really unfortunate. But what am I gonna do about it?

Doesn't your writing, perhaps even more dramatically than we discussed before, serve as a kind of self-exploration: Who am I? Where do I come from?

That as well, of course. I already said it, I want to know: Why am I here? And generally: What's it all good for?

And what is it all good for?

Read my books, I am not able to tell you more precisely than I do in them. In plain terms, I am here to cause a bit of a ruckus. I am here to lift the mood a bit. I am here to see to it that there is a bit of awareness. I am here so that some people, including me, will maybe suffer a bit less from the sleeping sickness they are already suffering from. And I will only be able to keep this up for a little while and then I just won't be able to anymore.

Has being Jewish shaped your self-conception and your work?

Well, you're saying that quite lightly. I would begin by arguing about the question whether I am a Jew or not. It is without question that my parents were Jews. But I find it interesting to ask whether people whose parents were Jews are actually Jews as well. That was the opinion of the authors of the Nuremberg Race Laws, for example. It is also the opinion of Orthodox Jews. But I somehow wish I could choose for myself. It's not that I am trying to hide it. Look at my books, they're full of it. But I want to be able to choose who I am. I know that this is only possible to a certain extent and I also know that, whether you want to be or not, to an extent, you are what others think you are. There is no recourse from that. I am aware that what you call 'being a Jew' or Jewish culture, has played a role for me in many, many regards.

What is Jewish identity anyway?

I am far from being able to answer that question. I know it is a national sport in Israel and that many people in Brooklyn concern themselves with it. As soon as two Jews get together, they start talking about it. I am not permanently searching for my identity. I know that I would be a completely different person had I not had this specific origin. I would have completely different tastes, other preferences, a different idea of justice, of language, of telling stories, of humour, of God knows of what. That's without question. The question is whether that means 'being Jewish'. You could say, yes, it does. You could also say, no, it doesn't. You could say you don't know.

Were you ever discriminated against because of your Jewish heritage?

Perhaps I was lucky or maybe it was a coincidence or maybe not, but I never had to deal with anti-Semitism or anti-Semitic behaviour toward myself. Never, not for a second. Neither in the GDR, nor since I lived in the West, since 1977. Although I do not feel a hundred percent Jewish, my reaction to it would be that of a person who is two hundred per cent Jewish. And I wait to encounter those instances of anti-Semitism. Well, I don't wait, but I think that, if it came down to it, I would meet them with a loaded gun.

So, I cannot imagine that I am someone who would just suffer quietly and take it. In my opinion, the only appropriate reaction to anti-Semitism is aggressiveness. There is no other method as far as I'm concerned. There is no other method that preserves a certain measure of dignity. And I cannot imagine confronting manifestations of anti-Semitism with benevolence or understanding or forgiveness. I do not want to concern myself with the reasons for anti-Semitism. I don't care. The reasons are well-known. They are, so to speak, thought through. It's not a forum where one can demonstrate the depth of one's insight.

You lived in the GDR for many years. How was your time there? Did you feel controlled and restricted?

All in all, my time in the GDR was good. For a long time I was what you would call a convinced socialist and I was sure of the fact that, in the GDR, they were making an effort for the cause. When it occurred to me that the way in which this effort was made was disastrous, I began to distance myself from the GDR. Okay, certainly we can argue whether this suspicion came to me curiously late in the game. Either way, it did not come to me until it came. And that was around the time when Warsaw Pact troops entered Czechoslovakia in 1968. Until that point I was surfing the wave of acquiescence, so to speak. I only became a writer after that. And it is true that the more of a writer I became, the more constrained I felt. This might surprise you, but I left the GDR more for private than for political reasons. I am not talking about some affair with a woman here. I am talking about my relationship with my work. Toward the end of my time in the GDR, I was very agitated and only reacted. My writing began to resemble a kind of nervous barking. And I looked at it and it was not consistent with my idea of literature and I had to ask myself whether being a writer is the same as being a resistance fighter. And it's not the same. I had to choose one of the two careers. For example, back then, when I thought of a story like the dismay you feel over your first heartache—I am making this up now—or the feeling you get when a woman puts her hand on your shoulder in a certain light, in a certain place—if I had wanted to write this back then, I would not have dared. I would have been afraid of everyone thinking: Now he's given up. Now they broke him.

You wanted to get out of this dilemma?

. . . Yes, the reason I am telling you this is to demonstrate how conditioned I was, that I was driven, that I was not able to do what I wanted, but basically had to do what was expected of me. And I left the GDR mainly in order to escape this situation. I just wanted to write about that hand on my shoulder without having to be ashamed. I didn't go straight to West Germany. First I went to the United States for a while. I had a guest professorship there and my plan was to stay until I was no longer a political enemy, but a literary enemy.

How long were you in America?

Four years. Not all at one time, but I went there off and on as a visiting professor.

You were allowed to leave the GDR?

Yes, it was a privilege granted to me for being a successful writer, and that's what I meant when I said that *Jacob the Liar* made my life very comfortable.

How do you feel about the country that granted you these privileges today?

The past is the past and no one is going to change it. Of course it all could have gone differently, of course I would have liked it to be different. I would have wished for the GDR to be more of a success. I would have wanted to see it managed less poorly, so that things might not have been so thoughtless and so crude and untruthful and corrupt. It is no great pity that the GDR perished. The GDR that existed didn't deserve otherwise. What I do feel sorry for is the fact that what the GDR could have been in my eyes also perished. The past is also the German unification.

That was managed poorly too. That could have been done better too, but so it goes. When something's been messed up, it's messed up. An escaped horse is an escaped horse. Now we just have to see how to get it back.

Translated by Jonathan Becker

ACKNOWLEDGEMENTS

Jurek Becker published his first collection of essays and speeches under the title *Ende des Größenwahns* [Ending Delusions of Grandeur] in 1996, a year before his death. About 10 years later, at the suggestion of his publisher, Suhrkamp Verlag, I began to sift through my husband's literary estate to add further essays, speeches and interviews to his original selection. In 2007, the new edition was published under the title *Mein Vater, die Deutschen und ich* [My Father, the Germans and I]—inspired by Becker's speech *Über Deutschland* [About Germany], which had been reprinted under this very title.

For the volume at hand, the first English language edition of Jurek Becker's essays, a selection was made based on the second German edition. Several of its essays had already been published in English, so an interest in these texts was apparent in the English-speaking world.

In selecting the remaining texts for translation, I was advised by the American translators Martin Bäumel and Tracy Graves. Together we chose texts that were representative of the author's engagement with politics, society and the cultural life of his time. In this book, these essays appear in chronological order, because they frequently refer and react to contemporary political events.

The following index contains specific information about the time and occasion of each text's conception. I have also included publication information for those English translations that have already appeared elsewhere. Many of the texts in the volume have a lengthier publication history, having appeared in German in both books and various periodicals. For reasons of clarity, I have omitted details about the original German publication here.

We have made every effort to resolve all issues of rights. However, we ask those who believe to have justified claims to contact the publisher.

Christine Becker

My Way of Being a Jew was written for a serial programme of the German radio station *Süddeutscher Rundfunk* in 1977. The English translation appeared in 1978 in *Dimension. Contemporary German Arts and Letters* (Austin, Texas).

Writers East and West, a lecture given at University College of London in 1979, has never before been published in English.

Resistance in 'Jakob der Lügner', written for a colloquium at the University of Toronto, was originally published in English in *Seminar: A Journal of Germanic Studies* (Toronto, Canada) in 1983.

The speech *On the Decline of Culture in Our Times* was delivered on the occasion of the *Römerberggespräche* (a serial of debates on social issues) in Frankfurt am Main, in 1983. It has never before appeared in English translation.

On the Value of Civil Rights was written for a conven-
tion of the German Union of Educators and Scientists
(*Gewerkschaft Wissenschaft und Erziehung*) in 1983
on the occasion of the protest against the deployment
of nuclear missiles in Germany. The speech has never
before been published in English.

This Is Unreliable Information, a conversation with
Marianna Birnbaum, then Professor of Hungarian
Studies at the University of California, Los Angeles,
was originally published in English as *An Interview
with Jurek Becker*. It appeared in *Cross Currents: A
Yearbook of Central European Culture* (Ann Arbor,
Michigan) in 1989.

Is Socialism Over and Done With?, an article written
in response to a question posed by the German weekly
journal *Die Zeit* in October 1989, has never before
been published in English.

The State of Europe was written in response to a
request by *Granta* magazine. In December 1989, the
editors of *Granta* asked a number of writers to reflect
on the dramatic changes taking place in Central and
Eastern Europe. The text originally appeared in
English in *Granta* (Cambridge, UK) in 1990.

The Invisible City was written for the catalogue
accompanying the exhibition *Unser einziger Weg ist
Arbeit* [Our Only Chance is to Work] (1990), which
displayed photographs taken in the Łódź ghetto
between 1940 and 1944. The essay has never before
been published in English.

It Takes Two to Spy was written during the debate on how to deal with East Germany's past and was originally published in the German weekly journal *Die Zeit* in 1990. It has never been published in English.

On the Tools of Writers, a speech given in Neumünster on the occasion of the acceptance of the *Hans Fallada Prize* in 1990, has never before appeared in English.

On Germany, a speech delivered in Weimar in 1994, was published in German under the title *Mein Vater, die Deutschen und ich* [My Father, the Germans and I] in *Die Zeit*. It was published in English in *Dimension. Contemporary German Arts and Letters* (Austin, Texas) in 1994.

The Centipede, delivered at a symposium on multiculturalism in contemporary German literature at Washington University in St Louis, was published in English in *World Literature Today* (Norman, Oklahoma) in 1995.

It Is Like a Thunderstorm, a conversation with photographer Herlinde Koelbl, was originally recorded for Koelbl's book *Im Schreiben zu Haus* [At Home in Writing], published in 1998. It first appeared in Germany's weekly magazine *Der Spiegel* in March 1997. It was the author's final interview.

1937

Born in Łódź (Poland) as son of Jewish parents, Jurek Becker spends most of his early years in the Łódź ghetto and in the concentration camps at Ravensbrück and Sachsenhausen.

1945

Becker's mother dies in Sachsenhausen shortly after the liberation. His father moves to Berlin and Becker begins to learn German.

1955

Becker finishes Gymnasium. Subsequently, he spends two years in the East German Armed Forces. He then begins his study of philosophy at the Humboldt Universität in East Berlin.

1960

After he is expelled from the university for political reasons, Becker becomes a freelance writer. His early projects include screenplays for film and television and texts for political cabaret.

1961

Jurek Becker marries Erika Hüttig and their first son Nikolaus is born.

1964

Son Leonard is born.

1969

Becker publishes his first novel *Jacob the Liar*. *Jacob the Liar* has been translated into more then twenty languages and adapted for film in both East Germany (*Jakob der Lügner*, 1975, dir. Frank Beyer) and Hollywood (1999, dir. Peter Kassovitz).

1973

Becker's second novel *Misleading the Authorities* is published in the German Democratic Republic and the Federal Republic of Germany.

1976

The Boxer is published in East and West Germany. *The Boxer* has appeared in translation in several languages and has also been made into a film (1980, dir. Karl Fruchtmann).

Becker signs the petition against the expatriation of singer and writer Wolf Biermann. As a consequence, he is expelled from the Socialist Party and removed from the executive committee of the Writer's Association.

1977

Frank Beyer's screen adaptation of *Jacob the Liar* is awarded the Grand Prize of the Jury at the Berlin

International Film Festival and is nominated for an Oscar for Best Foreign Film.

Becker leaves the Writer's Association. His divorce from Erika Hüttig is finalized in April.

After refusing to accept the East German government's censorship of his most recent novel, *Sleepless Days*, he moves from East to West Germany in December.

1978
Becker spends the spring semester at Oberlin College in Oberlin, Ohio.

His novel *Sleepless Days*, which was declined publication permission in the GDR, is published in the West and later adapted for film in West Germany (*Sleepless Days*, 1982, dir. Diethard Klante) and in reunified Germany (1991, dir. Gabriele Denecke).

1980
After the First Future, a collection of short stories, is published in the West. The collection includes the novella *The Wall*, which was later made into a movie by director Frank Beyer.

1982
The novel *Everybody's Friend* is published in West Germany. The following year, an East German edition is permitted as well.

1983
Becker is elected to the *Deutsche Akademie für*

Sprache und Dichtung (Academy of Language and Poetry) in Darmstadt.

1984
During the spring semester, Becker gives lectures at Cornell University in Ithaca, New York.

1986
Bronstein's Children is published in East and West, translated into several languages and later made into a movie starring Armin Mueller-Stahl. The TV series *Liebling Kreuzberg*, for which Becker has written, is aired. It becomes one of the most popular series on German TV and Becker receives several prizes for it later on. Becker marries Christine Harsch-Niemeyer.

1987
Becker spends the fall semester at the University of Texas in Austin, Texas.

1989
Becker holds the guest lectureship in poetics at the Johann Wolfgang Goethe-University in Frankfurt am Main. His lecture series is published the following year.

1990
Son Jonathan is born. Becker becomes a member of the *Akademie der Künste* (Academy of the Arts) in Berlin.

1992
The novel *Amanda Heartless* is published and afterwards translated into several languages.

1993

Becker spends the spring semester at Washington
University in St Louis, Missouri.

1996

A collection of essays, lectures and interviews titled
Ending Delusions of Grandeur is published.

1997

Jurek Becker dies in Schleswig-Holstein, Germany.